POLICE HEROES

Allan Zullo

SCHOLASTIC INC.

To all law enforcement officers who have chosen to put their lives on the line for the safety and protection of us all, and to those badge-wearing heroes who gave the ultimate sacrifice while carrying out their duties serving our communities.
—A.Z.

ISBN 978-1-338-08810-6

10 9 8 7 6 5 4 3 2   17 18 19 20 21

Printed in the U.S.A.   40
First printing 2017

Book design by Cheung Tai

ACKNOWLEDGMENTS

I wish to thank all the law enforcement officers featured in this book for their willingness to recall details and answer questions in lengthy, personal interviews with me about their heroic actions.

My appreciation extends to the media representatives of various police departments who provided me with important contact information and, in some cases, helped set up interviews. They are Jan Caldwell, media relations director, San Diego County Sheriff's Department; Lieutenant Jeff Gordon, public information officer, North Carolina State Highway Patrol; Ryan Larrondo, public information specialist, Boise Police Department; Stephen McCausland, public information officer, Maine State Police; Captain Angelo Nieves, unit commander, and Jeff Williamson, both of the public information office, Orange County Sheriff's Office; Joseph Pentangelo, media relations representative, the Port Authority of New York & New Jersey; and the press information office of the Georgia State Patrol.

CONTENTS

TO SERVE AND PROTECT

For the more than 900,000 sworn law enforcement officers in our country, being a member of the front lines of justice is more than a job. It's a calling. They take seriously their oath to uphold the laws of the land and to serve and protect the people of their city, their county, or their state—even at the risk of their own life and limb. And we're all safer because of them.

They are the ones who deal with the worst of humanity so that the rest of us don't have to, which often means going into places where no one else will go and doing the necessary things that no one else will do.

They are the ones summoned when a drunken parent hurts his family, when a car wreck takes the life of a texting teenager, when a burglar breaks into a house and steals a cherished family heirloom.

They are the ones who search for and find a toddler missing in the woods, who do CPR on a heart attack victim at the scene of an accident, who pluck a mother and child out of a flooded culvert.

They are the ones who go down a dark alley in search of a murder suspect, who bust into a house of armed drug dealers, who rescue hostages from a homicidal prison escapee.

Rank-and-file cops ride emotional roller coasters on tracks that twist and turn from stress and satisfaction to joy and heartbreak. During a shift, they might handle a fender bender, settle a heated dispute between neighbors, and then skip the rest of their lunch to chase after a purse snatcher.

When police officers solve crimes or comfort victims, they are lucky if they receive a thank-you. During an arrest, they may get yelled at or spit on, sometimes by onlookers—the very people they are trying to serve.

And then there are those moments—fortunately, rare— when police officers must whip out their firearms, point them at someone, and decide in a split second whether it's a life-and-death situation that requires pulling the trigger.

Police officers must prepare for their own deaths every day. After they put on their bulletproof vests, secure their weapons to their duty belts, and say good-bye to their families, they leave home without knowing who or what they will encounter on their shift—or even if they will make it home alive. We will never forget the 60 brave law enforcement officers—37 from the Port Authority Police Department and 23 from the New York Police Department—who lost their lives on 9/11.

In 2016, according to the Officer Down Memorial Page, 132 police officers died in the line of duty, including accidents.

Among the fatalities that year were 74 officers killed by criminals. The year before, 56 officers perished in felonious acts perpetrated by bad guys. Based on the statistics of line-of-duty deaths during the five-year period from 2011 to 2015, a police officer dies on the job in our country about every two and a half days. On average, during a typical week, 1 cop gets murdered and 302 more are victims of criminal assaults, including approximately 266 attacks that cause serious injury.

In recent years, with the growing number of cell phones and body cameras recording police encounters, we have seen shocking examples of police misconduct, sometimes leading to unwarranted deaths. What we seldom see highlighted in the media, however, are the 99.99 percent of dedicated law enforcement officers who day in and day out do the right thing. They make our streets safe, go the extra mile to resolve an issue, and protect our rights, freedoms, and security. Every day, committed officers do great things that we never hear about—but even if we did, we might take them for granted.

This book features 10 compelling stories about ordinary law enforcement officers who, powered by extraordinary courage or compassion or both, gave everything they had—and then some—in heroic efforts that saved lives, prevented tragedies, or eased heartache in a time of despair. They were all quite humble and quick to give credit to their training and their comrades. Among the heroes you will read about are the big-city officer who endangered his own life to stop others from ending theirs, the patrolmen who raced through a deadly wild-fire to evacuate dozens of homeowners, the small-town cop who single-handedly ended a murderous rampage, the female deputy who was shot seven times while saving the lives of three children, and the state trooper who sacrificed his cruiser to stop a wrong-way driver from a head-on collision.

None of these heroes did it for the medals and honors they received afterward. They did it because that was what they were trained to do, what they needed to do, what they wanted to do. It was their job. It was their calling.

TAKING IT THE WRONG WAY

TROOPER DOUGLAS CROPPER
Maine State Police

When an elderly man drove past Trooper Douglas Cropper going the wrong way on a busy interstate highway, the officer pictured what would likely happen if he didn't stop the wayward motorist in time: Innocent people would be maimed or killed in a high-speed, head-on collision.

Cropper's cruiser was on the shoulder, pointing with the flow of traffic. Not willing to turn around and drive against oncoming vehicles that were clipping along at 50–60 miles an hour, the seasoned trooper knew exactly what he needed to do. His plan would be perilous and would put him in harm's way, but it was his best option—really, his only option—if he was going to prevent a horrible tragedy.

The trooper intended to race ahead of the car and then sacrifice his police cruiser and risk possible injury to himself by causing the two vehicles to crash. What preyed on the trooper's mind were two worrisome questions that would be answered in the next few heart-pounding minutes: Could he intercept the car in time to avoid a likely deadly pileup with other vehicles? And if so, would he and the old man be hurt or killed in the two-car wreck that he was deliberately about to cause?

Cropper knew every square foot of pavement along the 30-mile section of I-295 in Maine from South Portland to Brunswick because he had been patrolling it for years. On this bustling four-lane stretch of urban highway that sliced through the city of Portland, he had pulled over countless drunk drivers and speeders, chased bad guys, and responded to everything from fender benders to fatalities.

In 2005, he engaged in a dangerous chase that reached speeds of 130 miles an hour before he apprehended the suspect safely. On Easter Sunday 2010, on this same section, Cropper found himself in another wild chase after a driver sped off over a simple seat belt violation. The trooper pursued the suspect, who streaked off I-295 and into a neighborhood where he bailed out of his car. With Cropper tailing him on foot, the guy sprinted to a residence but couldn't get the front door open. The trooper, who had played tight end on the football team at Springfield College in Massachusetts, tackled the man and, after a brief scuffle, arrested him. Cropper discovered the suspect was a member of an outlaw biker gang and a felon driving with a revoked license.

On June 29, 2012, the veteran 41-year-old trooper was working his territory in an unmarked, gray Ford Crown Victoria. Nothing was happening out of the ordinary, just the usual number of violators deserving tickets. By the afternoon,

I-295 traffic through Portland began building up—it was the Friday before July Fourth—but people were still speeding, and he was still nabbing them.

Shortly before 4:00 p.m. on the expressway, just a few feet past the Exit 6A off-ramp, Cropper pulled over the driver of a box truck for going 69 miles an hour in a 50-mile-per-hour zone. With the vehicle on the shoulder of the right-hand southbound lane, the trooper took the trucker's driver's license and logbook and walked back to the police cruiser to fill out the paperwork.

While Cropper was completing the task in his car, a call came in from dispatch, which had "Gray" as its call sign. Referring to the officer's number, dispatch said, "Gray, 135."

"Go ahead, Gray."

"You've got a silver 2010 Toyota Corolla going northbound on the southbound lane from Exit 5. Elderly man driving."

"Ten-four," Cropper said, using police radio lingo for "I understand the message."

As soon as he hung up, the trooper noticed southbound traffic slow down. Brake lights flashed, and vehicles in the passing lane suddenly moved over to the right-hand lane, including a tractor-trailer. After the semi passed him, Cropper noticed the Corolla going north in the southbound passing lane.

I've got to flag him down, the trooper thought. Exiting his car, Cropper ran out into the highway, barely paying attention to the vehicles that were braking behind him.

Cropper jumped up and down, waved his arms at the driver of the Corolla, and yelled, "Stop! Stop! You're going the wrong way!" But the elderly man behind the wheel made no attempt to slow down or pull over. He drove past Cropper and kept heading north at about 45 miles an hour as southbound cars veered away from him.

Over the years, Cropper had dealt with wrong-way drivers. One time, a puzzled old lady drove into a construction site on I-295 in broad daylight. The trooper managed to stop her without incident. Another time, a drunk driver headed northbound in a southbound lane and kept going even after Yarmouth police used a spike strip to puncture his tires. Cropper, who was going southbound, received a nice scare when the drunk nearly collided head-on with him before stopping.

Then there was that terrible rainy night in 2006 when the trooper was training a new officer. They had arrived at the scene of a wreck on I-295 near Tukey's Bridge. As he stepped out of his cruiser, Cropper spotted a Toyota RAV4 going northbound in a southbound lane. Cars were swerving to avoid a collision, causing traffic to bunch up. On the other side of the median, a Portland police officer was driving with traffic on the northbound lanes, going parallel with the motorist—later identified as an 84-year-old retired truck driver. The cop used the squad car lights and siren and pointed a spotlight at the errant driver trying to get his attention, to no avail.

The elderly man drove the wrong way for more than two miles on the interstate until his vehicle collided head-on with a midsize car driven by a retired educator near the Lunt Road overpass in Falmouth. The oblivious driver was killed instantly, and the other motorist died after being transported to the hospital. Both persons were alone and not wearing seat belts.

Cropper arrived moments after the horrific crash, which left the vehicles mangled beyond recognition. A short while later, the trooper had the gut-wrenching duty of informing the next of kin of the death of the innocent motorist. Cropper had delivered similar heartbreaking news to victims' relatives many times. It was always difficult to do. On this night, he drove to a house in South Portland to inform a woman that her husband had died in a wreck through no fault of his own. Cropper learned that the victim had been a recently retired dean of students who was on his way home from L.L. Bean's flagship retail store in nearby Freeport, where he worked part-time to make a little extra spending money.

Later, Cropper watched the Portland police officer's dash-cam cam video of the futile chase: the wrong-way car causing more than 30 oncoming vehicles to swerve . . . the cop doing all he could to make the motorist stop . . . the unsuspecting retired educator failing to react in time . . . and the two vehicles slamming into each other with such force they both flew into the air. The image of that violent 2006 crash had remained etched in Cropper's mind for years, stored in what he called his "knowledge box."

Now it was six years later, and an almost identical situation was unfolding about five miles south of that double fatality on the same highway. From experience, Cropper figured the befuddled driver would do one of four things: stop and pull over once he realized he was going the wrong way; turn at the next exit against traffic; use the next crossover (an opening in the median reserved for emergency vehicles only) and head the correct way; or cause a crash, perhaps involving multiple cars, that seriously injures or kills him and others.

As the trooper sprinted back to his cruiser, he was committed to preventing that last possibility.

I have to stop him before he nears the bridge, Cropper thought. The rogue car was traveling toward a treacherous section of the highway about two miles away, just south of Tukey's Bridge. Because of the road's curves and rises near the bridge, Cropper worried that southbound drivers would find it difficult, if not impossible, to have enough time to recognize and react to the danger of the wrong-way Corolla.

He never considered trying to catch up with it by driving north through southbound traffic. That was out of the question. He decided there was only one way to stop the motorist from crashing into others—the trooper needed to crash into him first. This meant Cropper would have to speed in the northbound lanes and beat the driver to the nearest crossover, which was a mile away, just past Exit 7, and a mile south of Tukey's Bridge. Then the trooper would have to turn into the crossover and nudge his cruiser into the Corolla's lane to ram the car or cause it to ram into him.

This was a dicey tactic with no guarantee that either person would be spared injury or death. But Cropper felt he had no other choice. He had to act fast, aware that every second mattered.

Because the interstate was divided by a wide median protected by guardrails, he couldn't simply drive across the median, make a U-turn, and head north in a northbound lane. He would have to take the off-ramp, go under the I-295 overpass, then turn onto the on-ramp and zoom north to the crossover.

Back in his cruiser, Cropper buckled his seat belt and turned on the siren and two blue lights on his dashboard. "Gray, he just went by me," Cropper radioed dispatch. "I tried to stop him, and now I'm going after him. I'll try to beat him to the crossover after Exit 7."

The driver's license and logbook of the trucker he had stopped minutes earlier were still sitting on the front seat of his Crown Vic. Cropper couldn't afford to waste even the few seconds it would take to return them. With the hapless trucker wondering where the trooper was going with the important items, Cropper backed up about 100 feet along the shoulder to Exit 6A and squealed down the off-ramp and onto Forest Avenue. He went under the overpass, expecting to immediately enter the northbound on-ramp.

To his dismay, orange and white barrels blocked entry to the ramp because it was undergoing major reconstruction. He looked at the other northbound on-ramp. It was blocked off, too. He uttered a few choice words out of anger and frustration and felt his heart beating faster. *Of all the times for the ramps to be closed . . .*

Now it would take even longer to reach the crossover because he would have to weave his way along surface streets to the next interstate on-ramp at Exit 7, about three-quarters of a mile away. *Do I have enough time?* he wondered.

Up ahead, at the next intersection, he needed to turn left onto Marginal Way, a street parallel to I-295. The light was green. *Please stay green,* he thought. If it turned red, he would have to slow down and make sure the intersection was clear before proceeding. He couldn't afford to lose even a second.

As he approached the intersection, he was relieved to see the light remained green. But several cars were ahead of him in the left turning lane. *I'll have to turn left from the right-hand lane,* he told himself. Drivers are taught that they should generally move to the right for emergency vehicles that are running with their sirens and lights on. But in this case, Cropper hoped that those in the left turning lane would stay put. This was no time for drivers to move into his lane.

Fortunately, none did. The trooper made a wide left turn from the right lane onto Marginal Way—a busy commercial two-way street with center turn lanes—and headed north. As he neared a well-used crosswalk, he was thankful no one was in it. *Good,* he thought. *Now it's just a straight shot to Franklin and onto the ramp. But can I make it in time?* He pressed his foot harder on the accelerator.

As he picked up speed, he encountered drivers who weren't reacting quickly enough to get out of his way. He was forced to steer his hurtling Crown Vic over the yellow center line and into the southbound center turning lane. As he neared the next intersection, he again tried to will the traffic light to stay green. It remained green, but he had to slip through a space between a car in the left turning lane and a car in the northbound lane.

His main concerns were his safety and the safety of others on the surface streets. Sure, he had both his dashboard blue lights flashing and his siren blaring, but he was driving a stealth car, not an easily recognized marked police cruiser with a bar of blue lights on the roof. The trooper worried there might be a driver who wasn't paying attention or didn't realize the speeding gray vehicle was a cop car.

His eyes constantly darted left, right, forward. His hands gripped the steering wheel, poised to react to any possible situation, such as dodging startled pedestrians, passing slow-poke vehicles, or veering around cars that might pull out from side streets and into his path.

Cropper knew he had no control over what the wrong-way driver was doing on I-295. But he had control of himself on Marginal Way. *I must make sure I don't hurt anyone. If I crash now, I'm out of the game, and the wrong-way driver will keep on going until he crashes.*

The trooper gunned the engine, but the driver of a dark minivan was apparently unaware of the siren and flashing blue lights because the vehicle didn't move out of the way. Cropper was forced to steer his speeding northbound Crown Vic over the double-yellow center line and into the southbound center turning lane.

To his surprise, he approached a pedestrian island that was under construction. *Whoa! When did they start building that?* He swerved to the left and onto the lone southbound lane. Even though he was speeding the wrong way, he didn't face any oncoming vehicles for the next several hundred feet.

He moved back to his proper northbound lane, but traffic became so backed up that he had to return to the wrong side of the yellow line. By now, he was encountering several southbound vehicles that were heading straight toward him. *Stay out of my way*, he thought. They did, hugging the curb to give Cropper the space he needed. The trooper zoomed past 10, 20, 30 northbound vehicles on his right as he approached Franklin Street. Once again, he wondered, *Will luck still be with me? Will the light stay green?*

It did. From the left side of the yellow line, he turned left onto Franklin and then made an immediate right onto the Exit 7 on-ramp. But a car in front of him at the base of the ramp failed to move over quickly enough, momentarily forcing Cropper to slow down and shout, "No! No! Get out of my way!" The trooper swerved to his left and then accelerated up the ramp and onto I-295.

He hoped the wrong-way motorist hadn't already crashed into somebody. *If he's still driving, is he too far ahead of me? Am I too late?* Cropper took a quick glance across the median at the southbound traffic and saw the Corolla. It was still heading north. *There he is! Great! I still have a chance to stop him.* But the wayward car was slightly ahead of him. *It's going to be close, awfully close. I have to make it to the crossover before he goes by it.*

If the Corolla beat him to the spot, Cropper would have to go through the curves and over the bridge to the next crossover past Exit 9, nearly a mile away. The highway was full of blind spots on this side of the bridge, so the odds that the errant car could make it that far without causing a massive, deadly accident were slim. For Cropper, it was pretty much now or never.

He grabbed his mic and said, "135 to Gray, I see the wrong-way driver. I'm going to try to take him out." He hung up the mic.

Traffic was heavy in both northbound lanes, so the trooper skirted over as far as he could to the left and squeezed between the guardrail and the passing lane. Now he was even with the Corolla. With the crossover only a few hundred yards away, the cruiser spurted ahead of the car.

Cropper needed to make a sharp turn into the crossover as fast as possible without fishtailing or losing control and then stick his car out far enough—but not too far—to cause a crash. *If I overshoot it, I might get T-boned and end up hurt pretty badly.* Cropper had worked plenty of crashes and knew that people are often seriously injured or killed when another vehicle plows into the driver-side door. As he neared the crossover, he said a little prayer: *God, don't let him hit me in the door.*

But there was another concern: Would the trooper cause innocent southbound drivers to crash into him?

The next few seconds were going to require all the driving skills that Cropper possessed. Timing was everything for this critical, difficult maneuver. There was no room for error, no time to make any adjustments.

Now the crossover was less than a hundred feet away. With a glance at his side-view mirror, he saw he had maybe a two- or three-second lead over the wrong-way driver. But then the trooper quickly came upon a white pickup in front of him. *No! Not now! Don't slow me down!* At the last possible moment, the truck moved out of the way.

Cropper swung hard left into the crossover with tires squealing, hit the brakes, and then expertly positioned the car about halfway into the southbound passing lane—exposing enough of the cruiser for the wrong-way car to hit. *WHAM!* The Corolla smashed into the front left side of the Crown Vic, ripping off the whole front end.

The trooper had beaten him to the spot with less than a second to spare.

The Corolla came to a grinding, screeching stop, still facing north but at an angle that blocked the passing lane. Its engine died, its front end was badly damaged, and the right front tire went flat. Southbound cars—including at least one that was only a second or two away from striking the Corolla head-on—braked, skidded, and veered off to avoid a serious chain reaction accident.

The impact jolted Cropper's whole body and strained his neck, but he wasn't injured. After taking a moment to collect himself, he thought, *I got lucky, real lucky.* The trooper's plan had worked to perfection, just like he had intended. He had sacrificed his cruiser to immobilize the wayward car. Best of all, he had stopped the Corolla without causing anyone else to wreck. *It's a miracle there were no other accidents. So many southbound cars managed to avoid hitting us.*

Cropper picked up the mic and called in a 10-50, police radio lingo for cruiser accident. After reporting that his car was involved in the crash but that he was okay, the trooper requested an ambulance because he wasn't sure if the other driver was injured.

Although he was starting to feel some pain from whiplash, Cropper got out of his car and went over to the Corolla to check on the elderly driver who also had stepped out. Concerned the man might be injured or wander into the slowed-down traffic, the trooper ordered, "Sir, get back in your car and sit down."

After the man complied, the trooper asked, "Are you okay?"

Looking stunned and bewildered, the man, 88-year-old Kenneth Gill of Scarborough, said he wasn't hurt. He had been driving with his seat belt on.

"Sir, do you realize you were going the wrong way?" Cropper asked. After Gill didn't respond, the trooper said, "You were heading north in the southbound lanes. Where were you going?"

"To pay my water bill."

"Where is that?"

"Waterville."

He's obviously confused, Cropper thought. Waterville was 80 miles north of Gill's home in Scarborough, a southside suburb of Portland.

Within a minute, fellow state police officers from Troop G-Turnpike (I-95) began arriving on scene to handle traffic control and clear the wrecked cars. A short while later, Cropper went to an urgent-care facility to check for any hidden injuries. Fortunately, he was fine. The trooper then worked the rest of his shift, which turned out to be relatively quiet.

When he returned to the state police barracks, Cropper was given a message to call James and Edris Chouinard, a married couple from Lewiston, Maine. When he phoned them, they became emotional because they wanted to thank him for saving their lives.

They told him that with Edris, 52, driving their 1984 Mercury Marquis, the twosome had been heading south on I-295 on their way to celebrate their twenty-sixth wedding anniversary. James, 53, said they had come off Tukey's Bridge and were unaware that Gill was driving north in their lane. "We would have gone head-on into the other car at 65 miles an hour," James told him. Their Mercury fishtailed as it stopped just short of Cropper's cruiser.

Edris told the trooper, "Every now and again, I keep crying about it. I'm just so glad we're alive. You saved our lives. You're awesome because you put yourself at risk to stop that driver. If you hadn't done that, we all would've died. You're a hero."

Cropper said a friend of the Gill family told him that on the day of the incident, the family had taken the keys to the Corolla away from the elderly man. So Gill walked to the Toyota dealership and convinced an employee to give him another set of keys. Gill then returned to his home, got into the car, and drove off.

Police believe Gill entered the interstate at Exit 5 in Portland and had been traveling the wrong way for about a mile before dispatch notified Cropper.

After the crash, the trooper did not ticket Gill. "I talked it over with my sergeant and the district attorney's office, and I didn't see any point in fining him," Cropper says. "However, we did send Maine's secretary of state an adverse driving report that described the incident, and the state suspended his license for good."

A few hours after the incident, the truck driver who had been stopped by Cropper just before the wrong-way drama began called the state police, wondering what happened to his driver's license and logbook. They were still in the trooper's car. Cropper gave the items to his sergeant who personally delivered them to the trucker's home with an explanation of why the trooper took off with them.

When local and national media reported the remarkable story of Cropper's heroics, someone posted this online message: "I saw that trooper driving like an idiot on Marginal Way, and I yelled at him as he went by. Then I got up on the highway and saw him go through the crossover and crash into the wrong-way driver. Little did I know that the trooper was driving that way to stop the wrong-way driver and save lives. I am sorry that I yelled at the trooper when he whizzed by me."

For his actions that day, in November 2012 Cropper was named the nation's Officer of the Month, a prestigious award that recognizes an officer who has gone above and beyond the call of duty, by the National Law Enforcement Officers Memorial Fund.

"This came down to an officer making a calculated, risky decision, knowing full well he's going to place himself in some amount of danger," Lieutenant Louis Nyitray of the Maine State Police told the media.

"I am lucky to be alive and in one piece," says Cropper, who was promoted to corporal in 2015. "I am extremely grateful that the old man didn't get hurt and no one else did, either. It could have been so much worse.

"Everything had to click to prevent a tragedy—and everything did. If the lights had been red and I had to slow down even for just a few seconds, I wouldn't have made it. If cars had gotten in my way and slowed me down, I wouldn't have made it. I'm not religious, but I believe someone was watching over me."

IN THE LINE OF FIRE

OFFICERS CHRIS DAVIS AND JASON ROSE
Boise (Idaho) Police Department

It was the perfect storm for a tragedy.

A raging wildfire powered by strong winds, high temperatures, low humidity, and bone-dry brush was roaring with a vengeance into a quiet, unsuspecting neighborhood in Boise, Idaho.

As the first two police officers to arrive at the horrific scene minutes before firefighters did, Chris Davis and Jason Rose began sprinting door-to-door, warning residents to flee. Putting their own lives in danger, the two cops burst into burning houses, ran half-blind through choking smoke, and leaped through flames that ultimately scorched their uniforms and seared their skin.

The pair kept up a torrid, frantic pace. Even when they were driven back or flattened by explosions, they refused to give up because so many lives were in peril, never mind their own.

It all started so fast and furiously.

In the early evening of August 25, 2008, a brisk northwesterly front whooshed into Boise, where temperatures had soared to an unbearable 105 degrees. The front's fierce winds rattled windows, which set off security alarms all over the city and kept policemen and firefighters busy.

When a tree branch fell on a power line, it triggered a series of electrical events that caused a malfunction on a pole miles away. Shortly before 7:00 p.m., hot molten metal from the pole's equipment fell onto dry cheatgrass in an open field and ignited it. Fueled by sagebrush and other flammable woody plants and fanned by gusts of 50 miles an hour, the blaze spread rapidly and raced toward Oregon Trail Heights, a subdivision nestled on a ridge above the fire-ravaged field southeast of downtown.

As the closest officer to the wildfire, Davis zoomed over to the development and turned onto Sweetwater Drive where the homes on the ridgeline were most vulnerable to being destroyed by the blaze. Black smoke was billowing over the neighborhood, and flames were charging up the ridge. Davis stopped his car, jumped out, and started alerting everyone within shouting distance to evacuate immediately. Then he began going door-to-door.

At the first residence on the ridgeline, the garage door was up and the homeowner was putting something in the back of his car. Davis ran in and yelled, "Get out now! Get out!" Davis looked out through the back window of the garage toward the ridgeline. All he could see was a solid sheet of flames. The man got in his car and squealed out of the garage just as the home burst into flames.

Davis dashed outside; by the time he reached his patrol car, the flames had climbed the back of the residence and were arching over the roof. Davis paused for a moment, riveted by the frightening sight. *It's almost like a tidal wave of fire.* There was nothing in his training that prepared him for this. Over his eight years on the police force, the 33-year-old officer had dealt with people trying to shoot him, stab him, and fight him. But this was so different. *What can you do about fire?* he asked himself. *This is a big monster that's going to destroy a lot of homes.*

Nearby, Rose, 36, also an eight-year veteran on the force, was heading home in his patrol car, planning to secure his four kids' backyard trampoline, which had blown into a neighbor's yard during a windstorm the previous year. As he pulled into his driveway on Aphrodite Court, he heard a tone alert on his radio. Dispatch reported that a brush fire had flared up at the corner of East Amity and South Holcomb Roads, was growing rapidly, and was heading in a southeasterly direction. *That's only a few blocks from here.* He sped over to Sweetwater Drive, which was engulfed in smoke and flames. *This doesn't look good.*

Rose whipped out his cell phone, called his wife, Teddy, and bellowed, "Grab the kids, grab the dog, and get out of the house and into the car! A wildfire is heading your way!" Then he hung up.

He stopped his cruiser in the middle of the street, hopped out, and got his first good look at the ferocious fire. He met up with Davis to assess the mounting crisis. The smoke had turned so dark and heavy that he couldn't even see his patrol car anymore—only the rotating roof lights. Pulling his T-shirt over his nose, Rose said, "This is going to be bad, real bad."

Evacuation was the only way to save lives. Knowing that firefighters and fellow police officers wouldn't be arriving for another few minutes, Davis and Rose agreed they would separately go into as many homes as possible—even if it meant breaking into them—and clear all rooms.

Outside, some people were scurrying around, almost in a panic. Others were seizing garden hoses and spraying their residences—as if it would do any good. Several people were standing in the middle of the smoke-filled street, not sure what to do. Already, vinyl siding was melting on some homes, a burning garage collapsed, and the cedar shake roofs of several houses were on fire.

After the two officers had each cleared a couple of dwellings, the first fire trucks arrived and firefighters began hooking up their hoses to hydrants. At the same time, more police officers showed up to help with evacuations in other sections of the development. Davis drove farther down Sweetwater and parked sideways to block off the street near Council Bluffs Way. He left the engine, flashing roof lights, air-conditioning, and radio on and hurried to the closest house, where the front looked fine, but the back was burning.

Running to the next dwelling, Davis noticed that several homes on the ridgeline acted as temporary firewalls by blocking some of the wind-driven flames that were coming up from the field. But other flames were shooting out between the houses and jetting across the street.

Within minutes, the fire had breached much of the ridgeline on the block. When Davis looked back at his parked car, it was surrounded by flames. The cruiser had only 5,000 miles on the odometer and still had that new car smell. *I'll never see that car again,* he thought. *It's a goner.*

After clearing two residences, Rose didn't get an answer at the door of the next house on the ridgeline. He pushed it open and charged inside. It was eerily calm and quiet compared to the noise from the wind and fire outside, which sounded louder than a speeding freight train. *The silence is weird,* he thought before shouting, "Boise Police! Anyone home?"

Even though he didn't get any response, he still searched each room. Glancing at a huge window that looked out over the valley, Rose saw nothing but smoke and flames. He scampered downstairs to a game room. *No one here.* Then he entered the garage and saw a car pulling away as the automatic door closed. *Good, they got out.*

He went back through the home toward the front door. Passing the big window again, he thought, *Uh-oh, it's really hot.* He could feel air pressure building in the supercharged heat. Because Rose wasn't aware that the residence was already fully engulfed in fire, he opened the front door, letting in fresh oxygen and creating a backdraft—a phenomenon in which a fire that has consumed all available oxygen inside suddenly explodes.

The house blew up. The force of the blast threw Rose about 20 feet and slammed him hard to the ground. The last time he had felt a body blow that hurt this much happened during childhood when he was kicked by a horse. For a brief moment, the cop lost consciousness. Then he heard, "Hey, Rose, are you okay?"

Looking up from his prone position, he saw Davis bending over and talking to him, but Rose couldn't understand what Davis was saying because his ears were ringing so loudly and his brain felt scrambled. Trying to regain his bearings, Rose mumbled, "Yeah, I'm okay."

After slowly rising, he checked himself over. He felt pain from flash burns on the back of his head and neck and smelled the stink of burned hair. The roof of his mouth had been singed from breathing in hot embers. His back hurt as if someone had pounded it with a sledgehammer, and he couldn't hear out of his left ear. The back of his polyester uniform shirt had melted.

"We have to move, or the flames will get us," Davis said.

Snapping out of his mental fog, Rose thought, *I don't want to burn up. I've seen what happens to people who die in fiery car crashes. It's not a good way to go.*

He shook off the painful effects of the blast and gazed at the residences torched by flames that were now jumping from roof to roof. He was getting angry—and resolute. *This is my neighborhood. These are my neighbors, my friends. Their kids go to school with my kids. No way am I going to let anybody die.*

By now it was pure chaos—dozens of firefighters battling house fires on the left and right, police evacuating residents block by block, anguished people fleeing on foot and in cars, flames rocketing 40 feet into the air, and stifling smoke blanketing everything.

It was so noisy that shouting was the only way to communicate. The deafening sounds made by the wind and blazing homes were punctuated by constant mini-explosions as car batteries, gas cans, tires, and propane tanks in barbecue grills blew up. Power lines toppled over, dropping live wires that sparked and set off fires in lawns and bushes. Rose watched in disbelief as a water heater exploded in a burning house and blasted straight up through the roof like a Roman candle before crashing to the ground.

Despite the difficulties, the two officers stuck to their plan: They went in Rose's cruiser for several hundred feet, stopped, got out, dashed through smoke and fire, and split up to enter different homes. If no one answered within a couple of seconds, they kicked the door open and barged inside, sometimes startling people who were watching *Monday Night Football* or eating dinner and unaware of the imminent danger. The officers also encountered residents who were taking their sweet time deciding what to take with them. Whenever that happened, Davis and Rose physically removed them. People were urged to seek refuge at hastily set-up evacuation centers at nearby Trail Wind Elementary and Les Bois Junior High.

Davis and Rose entered some dwellings that were unoccupied except for the owners' pets. The officers shooed dogs and cats out the door so at least the animals had a chance at survival. But some pets were so petrified they hid, while others felt threatened or protective and were poised to attack. In such cases, the officers left them behind but kept a door open for them to escape. The cops' scratched arms and hands confirmed the old adage that no good deed goes unpunished.

The acrid smoke and toxic gases caused by burning plastics, chemicals, and fabrics were playing havoc on Davis's lungs and eyes. He was having difficulty breathing, feeling as if he was inhaling superhot air from a giant heater. He could barely see through the smoke and was constantly wiping his irritated eyes.

At one house where no one answered, Davis kicked in the front door, rushed inside, and caught a glimpse of the residents leaving through the garage. Because his eyes were stinging, he wiped them on a white curtain, leaving black smudges from his sooty face and hands. *Oh, geez, I've ruined these people's curtains*, he thought. As he scooted out of the residence, it erupted into flames. There was no longer a reason to feel guilty about the curtains.

Twice when Davis was searching a house for any lingerers, he cleared a back bedroom only to step into the hallway where flames blocked his way, forcing him to leap through them to escape. The Boise police were trained to develop a certain mind-set to finish whatever the task, no matter how difficult. *Fight through this and keep doing my best,* Davis told himself. *If I die, I die. But I have to keep going. There's nothing else I can do other than what I'm doing.*

And so, with lives at stake, he charged ahead across the flames. Thinking of his wife, he told himself, *If Kerry saw what I'm doing right now, she'd be very angry.*

Rose hustled over to a middle-aged man who was standing in the front yard, holding a garden hose and spraying water on hot spots around his residence, which was in the direct line of the wildfire.

"You have to evacuate now!" Rose shouted.

"I'm not leaving my house."

"You have to. The fire has already burned down several homes, and it's coming this way. Look at my head. I've already been burned."

"I'm staying right here to fight the fire," the man declared, continuing to spray.

"You don't get it," Rose countered. "You can't put out a range fire like this with a half-inch garden hose. This blaze is huge!"

The man lay down the hose and said, "Okay, then I better go back into my house and get my things."

"There's no time!" Realizing that the man still didn't understand the magnitude of the growing disaster, Rose took a drastic measure to save the guy's life. The officer grabbed him by the collar, spun him around, and punched him in the face—but not too hard. "You need to go now!" Rose declared.

"Okay, I get it. I get it," the man said, backing away. "I'm leaving." Rose watched him get into his car and drive off.

At another residence where the roof was on fire, Rose ran inside and tried to reason with a man who didn't want to evacuate. So the officer seized the guy's wrist, twisted his arm behind his back, and rushed him outside. When the man saw that his home was indeed on fire, he muttered a few swear words, gave a nod of understanding to Rose, and hurried away.

Davis entered a house that had just caught fire and found a flustered man who said he couldn't leave because his wife was in the bedroom picking out clothes and shoes that she wanted to save. "Show me where she is," Davis said.

The man led him to the bedroom, where the woman was still selecting items. "Get out of the house!" her husband ordered her. "Get out of the house!" She refused to evacuate because she wasn't through deciding what to take. The two continued to bicker.

"You don't have time for this!" Davis shouted. "Your roof is on fire!" Then he clutched each one by the arm and shoved them out—but not before the woman scooped up her cat.

Emerging from another burning residence on the ridgeline, Davis faced flames that were roaring over the roof and onto the front lawn. Because the wind had shifted, he wound up trapped by the fire and heavy smoke. *I'll be burned alive if I stay any longer. I've got to make a run for it.* He pictured his wife, Kerry, and two young boys, ages three and six, and told himself, *I want to make it back to my family.*

Holding his breath, Davis sprinted between two burning homes, where fire shot out as if from a huge blowtorch. As he bolted across the street, trying to outrun the flames, he felt the intensity of the heat on the back of his legs and head. His uniform shirt was smoldering.

Davis reached a yard that, to his luck, was being watered by sprinklers. He doused himself and then pressed his back against a fence to snuff out his smoking shirt. Because he had on a bulletproof vest, most of the skin on his torso was protected. He washed his face in the spray of a sprinkler, which helped him see and breathe better.

Hoping that being wet would prevent his clothes and skin from burning, he booted open the front door of the next house, which was ablaze. As he scurried from room to room, the air temperature had risen so dramatically that all the moisture on his head and back evaporated.

Davis, who was a jogger, was starting to falter physically, feeling as though he had just "hit the wall" in a marathon. Evading flames, scuttling from one side of the street to the other, breaking down doors, pushing people out of their homes, and breathing in noxious smoke was taking a heavy toll on him. But he willed himself to persevere.

Leaving Sweetwater Drive, he joined his comrade in Rose's cruiser and rode a few hundred feet onto East Immigrant Pass Court, a cul-de-sac where more houses were threatened with destruction.

Rose ran up to Peter and Mary Ellen Ryder's residence, which sat on the ridgeline. Flames had already reached the couple's backyard. He banged on the front door, rammed it with his shoulder, and kicked it. But it wouldn't budge and no one answered. He hurried over to a front window, pounded on it, and yelled, "Anybody there?" Nothing.

Figuring no one was home, he scampered next door and helped the occupants evacuate. Then he met up with Davis in the smoke-shrouded street, pointed to the Ryders' home, and said, "I can't get the door open." The two officers raced over there and tried to force it open, but it remained locked. The house then caught fire.

Deciding to leave, Rose and Davis were crossing the front yard when they spotted the homeowner, Peter, running alongside his burning residence from the exposed lower level in the back. Seconds earlier, he had gone out to his backyard looking for the source of the smoke when the wildfire flared up so quickly that flames blocked him from returning inside. Now he was silhouetted against flames that were right behind him—so close, in fact, that his shirt was smoking. The officers stopped Peter, put him on the ground, and rolled him, smothering his burning shirt.

When Davis helped him to his feet, Peter shouted, "My wife! My wife is still in the house!"

While Davis escorted him across the street to firefighters, Rose tried to gain entry by going around to the rear of the dwelling, but fire drove him back. Once again, he banged on the front door, yelling, "Open up! Open the door!" He threw his body against it, but nothing he tried worked.

He went over to the front window, which had sheer curtains, and peered inside. All he could see was an outline of Mary Ellen standing inside. Pounding on the window, he shouted, "Get out! Get out!"

Suddenly, the curtains began melting, and seconds later, the interior erupted in fire. Rose watched in shock and horror as Mary Ellen screamed and fell to the floor in a room that was being totally consumed by fire.

Davis was running up the driveway when he saw, through the front window, Mary Ellen collapsing in the flames. "The house is going to explode!" he shouted to Rose. Davis turned his back, spread his feet, and braced himself. The home blew up with such force it reminded him of a bomb detonating.

Rose hustled over to Davis and, in a voice cracking with emotion, said, "The woman is still inside."

"There's nothing we can do, Rose," Davis said. "Even if we could break in, we'd die. You can't save her because the house is too far gone."

The two officers turned around to flee but stopped and stared in amazement at a towering sheet of fire curling over the dwelling and above both of them. It curved down to the opposite side of the street, where it ignited the neighbor's grass and lilac bushes in the front yard and then touched off that house.

To Rose, this glowing, yellow wave was like being in a surfing movie, only with fire. He was so hypnotized by the fiery spectacle that he momentarily forgot about his heartache over seeing a woman burn to death.

Davis gripped him by the arm and said, "Come on, we've got more houses to clear."

Minutes later, Rose saw flames creeping only feet away from his squad car. *I have to move it out of the cul-de-sac before fire destroys it.* Meanwhile, Davis, having just cleared a residence, needed to reach the cruiser. But the wind-whipped fire had cornered him. Once again, he was forced to plow through the fire. Jumping into Rose's patrol car, he barked, "Rose, let's get out of here!"

Rose put the car in reverse but braked when he realized the blaze had blocked their way out of Immigrant Pass Court. The other choice was to go forward onto a pedestrian path that linked the cul-de-sac with another cul-de-sac about 200 feet away. But fronting the pathway were concrete posts designed to block vehicles from driving on it.

I just watched a lady die in front of me, Rose thought. *Her house exploded. The house next to hers is on fire, and the flames are about to burn us up. We have to escape.*

He put the cruiser in drive and tried to ram his way through the barriers, but the vehicle became hung up on a post. By putting the car in reverse and drive several times, he rocked the cruiser free. Then he backed up to within a few feet of the fire and told Davis, "All right, dude, hang on!"

Throwing the gear in drive, Rose floored the accelerator. The patrol car sheared off the posts at the base and hurtled down the pathway to the next cul-de-sac, where the two officers started evacuating people.

Fortunately, the wind had changed direction, so the two officers were now on the fringe of the smoke and flames and away from the wildfire's destructive track. To Davis, it was like a different world, even though they were only a few hundred feet from the last dwelling that had exploded. For the first time since he entered the fire-ravaged area, he could see more than 10 yards in front of him. Although it was still smoky, the air was so much better. He could actually breathe without going into a coughing fit.

Rose looked at his watch. It read 7:24 p.m. He and Davis had been clearing houses and leaping through flames for less than a half hour. *How can that be?* Rose wondered. *It seems like we've been doing this for hours.* Certainly his body felt that way.

His thoughts then turned to his residence, which was only a few blocks away. *The way the fire is heading, it looks like I might lose my home and everything in it. Well, at least Teddy and the kids are safe.*

"Rose," said Davis, "let's go to your house and get your valuables and pictures."

"I don't care about any of that stuff," Rose said.

They drove to his home anyway to take a breather and check on their comrades who were evacuating that section. When the pair arrived, they noticed the siding on several neighbors' homes had been scorched.

But luck had blessed Rose. Incredibly, the offshoot of the killer blaze that was menacing that particular area had stopped its advance right behind the house across the street from Rose's home. He had a gutsy neighbor to thank for that. Before the fire had reached the street, the neighbor, who worked for the US Bureau of Land Management as a heavy equipment operator, had brought in a bulldozer. He courageously scraped a firebreak through the brush, depriving the blaze of the fuel it needed to continue its merciless onslaught.

At Rose's residence, the first thing the two officers did was guzzle water. In the bathroom, Rose looked in the mirror. Because of the soot, he had the face of a coal miner at the end of a double shift. He also saw clear streaks running from his eyes down his cheeks. *They're from tears. I must have been crying over the woman who died.*

After scrubbing his face, he washed the top of his singed head and noticed strands of burned hair falling out.

* * *

Davis was exhausted, having cleared nearly 20 houses, about the same as Rose. Davis had lost his voice from yelling at people to evacuate. His throat was raw, his eyes were red, and his stamina was sapped.

The back of his shirt had melted along with parts of his bulletproof vest, belt, and boots. The back of his neck was burned, too.

Davis walked back to the smoking ruins along Sweetwater Drive. In the spotlights erected by firefighters, he saw destroyed houses lying in charred rubble; shells of burned-out cars with melted tires sitting in driveways; blackened trees standing naked, their bark and leaves stripped by flames; and once-beautiful lawns now covered in ash. Firefighters were still putting out small pockets of fire. *It's like a plane has firebombed the neighborhood*, he thought.

Through the wisps of rising smoke, he saw a patrol car—its roof lights still flashing—idling in the middle of the street where he had left his cruiser. *It must be someone else's car,* he thought. *I'm pretty sure mine got burned up.* He strolled over to the vehicle, which was pockmarked with burned paint. The windshield was yellowed and darkened from intense heat, and parts of the plastic bumpers had melted. *Whose car is it?* He looked at the number painted on the side. *Forty-two? That's my car! I can't believe it survived—and it's still running!*

He opened the door and was struck by the disgusting odor of smoke and burned plastic. He was relieved to find his wallet, which he had left in the car, was still there intact. Sliding into the driver's seat, Davis discovered the air-conditioning and engine were still working. He headed to the temporary command post that had been set up at a soccer field a half mile away. During the ride, he had to stick his head out the window to see.

Because Davis was still having trouble with his throat, lungs, and eyes, he was ordered into an ambulance at the command post. He joined Rose and five other officers, who were experiencing similar health issues after helping to evacuate residents. On the way to the hospital, they shared an oxygen mask to help them breathe. Each person took a few breaths and then passed it to the next guy.

Rose, who stripped off his burned uniform shirt and gear, was not feeling well. When an EMT asked him to cough, Rose started hacking and couldn't stop coughing up black mucous. His blood pressure was dangerously high, and his oxygen level was much too low. In the emergency room, the doctor flushed ash out of Rose's ears and told him, "You have a partial rupture of your eardrum."

The officers remained in the hospital for several hours before they were released. Davis went to the police station, where he took off his uniform and threw it, his gun belt, and his boots into the Dumpster because he couldn't stand the smoky odor. After he showered twice to get the stink off him, he put on street clothes that he had in his locker and arrived home at around 4:00 a.m. He was totally spent.

So was Rose. Around 2:00 a.m., his sergeant drove him from the hospital to his car. On the way back, she took him to Sweetwater Drive, telling him, "You need to see this."

Viewing all the devastation, Rose muttered, "My God, it's like a war zone. It's surreal. It's a tragedy."

But it was a tragedy that would have been so much worse if it hadn't been for the heroic actions of the first two police officers to arrive on scene.

The blaze—one of the worst ever in Boise—claimed the life of one person, Mary Ellen Ryder, 56, a popular professor of English and linguistics, who was scheduled to teach her first class of the semester the following day at Boise State University. No other residents were injured, but 17 police officers, who were assisting with evacuations and traffic control, and one firefighter were treated for smoke inhalation at two local hospitals.

The fire destroyed 10 homes, significantly damaged 9 others, caused lesser smoke and fire damage to 30 residences, and spurred the evacuation of more than 100 people in Oregon Trail Heights and parts of the adjacent Columbia Village subdivisions. Damage was estimated at $7 million. More than 400 emergency personnel, including firefighters and law enforcement officers from towns as far as 60 miles away, ultimately responded to the scene.

For their bravery and help in saving lives, Davis and Rose were named Top Cops in 2009, a prestigious honor given by the National Association for Police Organizations, which recognizes outstanding acts of service and heroism. The State of Idaho also awarded the two with its Medal of Honor.

"We happened to be there at the right time," says Davis. "We were a small part of a whole team of police officers, firefighters, and paramedics."

Promoted to corporal, Davis is a full-time instructor of new officers in Boise's police academy. He's also in charge of firearms, instructs fellow officers in the use of force, and is on the SWAT team.

Trying to evacuate people in such difficult conditions left Rose so mentally and physically drained that he slept through most of the next three days. He also was treated for post-traumatic stress disorder.

Rose, who has permanent hearing loss in his left ear, has since been promoted to corporal. About the awards he and Davis received, he says, "There's nobody in our department who wouldn't have done the same exact thing we did if they were in our shoes."

He adds, "The awards were humbling, but they also made me feel guilty because I couldn't save Mrs. Ryder."

Neither Rose nor Davis had ever experienced anything like the Oregon Trail Heights fire. "It acted as if it was alive and breathing and had some kind of evil purpose," recalls Rose. Davis agrees, adding, the blaze "was like a dragon blowing fire at us out of every window and door."

"JENNIFER, GET READY FOR A GUNFIGHT"

DEPUTY JENNIFER FULFORD
Orange County (Florida) Sheriff's Office

It almost didn't seem real to Deputy Jennifer Fulford.

Here she was, crouched in the confines of a small garage, exchanging gunfire with two bad guys—one on her left and another on her right, both no more than eight feet away. She had already been shot several times in the arm and leg, and she was losing blood.

But there was no quit in the 31-year-old deputy, not when the lives of three innocent, helpless children were hanging in the balance so close to her.

Whirling and firing in one direction, then the other, Fulford continued to fend off her attackers. Unexpectedly, in this, the most intense and terrifying moment of her life, she experienced the strangest of sensations. Time slowed to a crawl, noise became muffled, and pain diminished. And even more peculiar, she had the feeling that she was outside her body watching herself fight for her life. But as weird as this seemed, she also had never been more mentally locked in, more confident, more primed to vanquish the gunmen. She knew exactly what to do and when to do it without hesitation.

This garage will not be the last thing I see in my life, she vowed to herself.

Fulford popped up and fired at the gunman on her right just as a bullet tore into her right shoulder. Her gun fell to the floor, and she was too wounded to pick it up with her shooting hand. That's when the assailant on the left drew a bead on her and squeezed the trigger.

On the morning of May 5, 2004, Fulford was riding shotgun in her squad car with Deputy Jason Gainor, a trainee who was behind the wheel. Fulford, a deputy for three years, was familiarizing him with the area they would be patrolling that day.

Shortly before 8:00 a.m., they heard a Code 3—emergency response with lights and siren—over the radio. The dispatcher said an eight-year-old boy had called from a cell phone to report that strange men were in the house with his mother. Because he was whispering and the reception was poor, the dispatcher couldn't get any information other than the address, which was in a somewhat sketchy residential neighborhood in Pine Hills, Florida, a suburb of Orlando, where crime had been on the rise in recent years.

Deputies Dwayne Martin and Kevin Curry, who had been assigned to patrol that area, radioed dispatch that they were responding to the call. Fulford left it up to Gainor to decide whether the two of them should go to the address, too. Even though the house wasn't in their patrol zone, Gainor radioed that they were heading there as backup.

The pair pulled up to a modest one-story stucco home with an attached two-car garage and a neatly manicured lawn. It was the only residence on the block with burglar bars on all the windows and the front door. A burgundy SUV with South Carolina license plates was parked in the driveway.

Fulford and Gainor walked over to Martin and Curry, who were talking to a woman in the front yard. There was no sign of the boy who had called 911. Seeing a female deputy, the woman turned to Fulford and said, "There are three men in my house, and I don't know what they want or why they are here."

Pressing her for more information, Fulford asked, "Do you know who they are?" When the woman just kept repeating herself, the deputy thought, *She sounds robotic. It's bizarre because she's not upset and is showing absolutely no emotion.* That raised the deputy's suspicions. *If men were in my house and I didn't know them, I'd definitely be acting differently. She's not willing to tell me what's going on, which means it's probably something illegal.*

Unable to get anything else out of her, Fulford told her to stand by the patrol car parked on the street. The four deputies decided not to enter the house because they didn't know who or what they would be facing. Curry radioed for a helicopter and a K9 unit for further backup. A fence bordered the back-yard, so Gainor and Curry took up surveillance positions on neighbors' properties, hoping to get a better view of the rear of the dwelling.

Fulford and Martin remained in the front yard when the woman, displaying emotion for the first time, cried out, "My babies! My babies!" She pointed to the garage, where the left door was closed and the right door was open, exposing a parked minivan inside. The woman said her three children were in the vehicle.

This changes things, Fulford thought. *All the strangers have to do is put the garage door down, and then we'll have a hostage situation. Who knows, they possibly could kill the kids.*

"I'm going in the garage to see if I can get those kids out of there," she told Martin.

Fulford approached the open garage door. Another vehicle, an SUV, was parked behind the closed left garage door. After entering the garage, she walked between the two vehicles and peered into a window on the driver's side. She saw two toddlers buckled into car seats in the third row. She didn't see their older brother—the one who made the 911 call—because he was curled up on the floor in the middle row, too frightened to move.

Fulford tried the side door and then the driver's door, but they were locked. There was no way the youngsters—twin girls about two years old—could unlock the door. And the boy was so paralyzed by fear that he couldn't help, either.

"The children are in the minivan, but the doors are locked," she hollered to Martin, who was standing in the driveway keeping an eye on the front door in case the men exited from there.

Seconds later, she heard agitated male voices coming from inside the house, but she couldn't make out what they were saying. *They're probably talking about what to do because they spotted us*, Fulford thought.

An interior door in the garage that led into the home faced the passenger side of the minivan. While Fulford was standing on the driver's side of the vehicle, the interior door burst open and a man, later identified as George Jenkins, 25, emerged from the house and fired four shots out the open garage door at Martin.

Struck in the left shoulder, Martin dodged the other bullets and rolled into a hedge to the left of the garage between it and a neighbor's house to escape the kill zone.

As soon as Fulford heard gunfire, she dropped to the garage floor and radioed on her shoulder mic, "Shots fired! Shots fired!" From her prone position, she couldn't see Martin and didn't know he had been hit.

Trapped, she told herself, *Jennifer, get ready for a gunfight.* She pulled out her weapon, a Glock 21 that held 14 rounds. Adrenaline was surging through her body. Her only protection was the body armor covering her torso. Now it was up to her courage and the lessons she had learned during training sessions to survive—and to protect the children.

Jenkins, who was apparently trying to reach his SUV in the driveway, stepped out of the garage. Hearing Fulford speaking into her shoulder mic, the six-foot, 275-pound criminal spun around and started shooting his 9-mm handgun while advancing toward her.

From the driver's side of the minivan, Fulford moved toward the rear of the minivan, leaned around the fender, and fired at him, using a two-handed grip on her weapon.

Jenkins's first few bullets missed, but one of Fulford's rounds hit him in the pelvic area. He staggered into the garage, leaned his back against the wall that separated the house from the garage, and slid to the floor. Even though he was in a seated position, he continued to fire.

At least he's not walking toward me anymore, thought Fulford as she ducked behind the rear left wheel well of the minivan. At first, she wasn't aware that another man, later identified as John Dzibinski, 26, had charged into the garage through the interior door of the house. Still crouched low to the floor, Fulford noticed movement near the front of the minivan.

Leaning across the hood, Dzibinski had a clear shot at Fulford and fired. She looked around to see if there was someplace she could find cover without running outside into the open, but there was none.

This can't be happening! she thought.

Fulford returned fire, so he stooped behind the vehicle. Now she was alternating between firing at Jenkins at the back of the minivan and Dzibinski at the front. During a brief pause in the shooting, Fulford realized that her legs, which were pulled up in front of her in a squatting position, had been hit several times by Dzibinski. But she barely felt any of the bullet strikes early in the gun battle. She was too focused on returning fire.

As she swiveled back and forth, firing in two different directions, the situation reminded her of a carnival sideshow shooting gallery, where ducks keep popping up—except this was no game. This was life and death. Spurred by her training, Fulford was doing whatever she could to keep the shooters at bay and prevent them from killing her and possibly the kids.

In the back of her mind, she thought about all the reasons why she needed to survive—her family, her fiancé, her impending wedding. *I have so much to live for—getting married and having kids. And I've spent too much time and money on my wedding preparations.* She had just paid for her wedding dress.

During training, deputies were taught the importance of their mind-set when it came to surviving a gunfight. Fulford was already a positive thinker and a determined woman. *Just because I'm shot doesn't mean I have to lie down and die,* she told herself. *That's not going to happen to me today.*

She kept firing until her magazine went dry. As she quickly reloaded, Fulford knew—she just *knew*—that she would survive. *I won't let them kill me,* she promised herself. *I'll get them before they can get me.*

During the battle in such tight quarters, her mind began playing tricks on her. The loud racket of guns firing, bullets ricocheting, and glass breaking barely registered in her ears. All action, all movement seemed to happen in slow motion.

Part of her brain processed the wild scene in a way that caused her to feel totally detached from herself, as if she were watching a movie or having an out-of-body experience. The rest of her brain was totally fixed on reacting to every move the bad guys made.

Even from his sitting position, Jenkins had a slight angle on her and continued to shoot, winging her in the arm. Twice, Fulford bobbed around the rear of the minivan, fired, and then ducked behind the wheel well. The third time she leaned out, she shot him in the chest. Seeing where the bullet went and how he slumped to the ground, Fulford was pretty sure she had killed him.

But a split second before she shot him, his last bullet struck the right-handed Fulford in her right shoulder. The bullet damaged the nerves so badly that she lost all feeling in that arm and dropped her Glock. Her arm was dangling by her side, dripping blood, too weak for her to lift the weapon with her right hand.

Without missing a beat, Fulford picked up the gun with her left hand. Even though it wasn't her dominant hand, she had taken extensive training in offhand, or weak-hand, shooting three months earlier. During her weak-hand development training, she had to hold a tennis ball in her right hand and learn to use her left hand to do everything one-handed, including reloading the magazine with the help of her shoe and the ground.

Now all that practice firing as a lefty needed to pay off to keep Fulford and the children alive. The mechanics of shooting were the same, but she was unable to support the weapon with her right hand. Even without a two-handed grip, which would have provided better accuracy and helped cushion the recoil, she felt confident shooting as a lefty.

Once again, Dzibinski jumped up by the hood of the minivan and fired several rounds before slipping back out of view. Then he tried to finish her off. When he stretched over the hood and fired, Fulford shot back. This time, her bullet ended up exactly where she had aimed—in his head. Dzibinski stumbled out of the garage and into the driveway, where Martin, from his defensive position off to the side, fired several rounds at him until the assailant collapsed for good.

The fierce gunfight was over. It had lasted less than a minute.

Not hearing any more gunshots, Fulford, on the floor and resting against the minivan, noticed bullet holes in the vehicle. Her heart sank. *There's no way the kids are okay in there.*

But she was too weak to stand up and check on them. She began assessing her injuries and saw a blood puddle forming at her feet, not only from her injured arm but from all her other bullet wounds. She couldn't tell how many times she had been shot; she just knew it was a lot. Because of the loss of blood, she began feeling light-headed and seeing stars. On the verge of blacking out, she told herself, *Stay awake, Jennifer, in case the shooter comes back. And there's still a third guy somewhere.* She struggled to remain mentally alert. *Don't pass out. Don't pass . . .*

"Jennifer! Jennifer! Are you okay?" Hearing Curry's voice snapped her back to consciousness. He kneeled by her, his arm propping up her head. When he and Gainor had heard the shots, they had rushed toward the garage, but by the time they had taken up defensive positions, the gunfight had ended. "Are you okay?" he repeated.

That's a stupid question, Fulford thought. She shook her head and mumbled no. *Why is he calling me Jennifer?* Everyone in the department who knew her always called her Jen.

Curry and Gainor picked her up. As they were carrying her out of the garage, she was thinking, *You know what happens when you get shot. You go into shock. So, Jennifer, you have to control your breathing and slow down your heart rate.* Every time she closed her eyes to concentrate on her breathing, Curry shouted, "Jennifer! Stay with us!" He didn't want her to lose consciousness because he was afraid she would never wake up.

They carried her to the end of the driveway and laid her down on the grass by her patrol car. A fire department ambulance was idling at the other end of the block. Curry radioed to dispatch, "Get the ambulance over here! Officer down!"

"Negative, negative," the dispatcher said. "The scene isn't secure." There was still a possible active shooter inside the house, so protocol prohibited firefighters from entering such a dangerous zone. By now, five cruisers had arrived, and deputies were setting up a perimeter around the house, waiting for the SWAT team to show up.

Determined to save time, Curry, Gainor, and several other deputies carried Fulford down the block to the ambulance. Because of the adrenaline, the real pain hadn't set in yet. Not that she cared. She was just relieved to be out of the garage and still alive. But she was worried about the fate of the children.

As Fulford was being rushed to the hospital, the paramedic in the ambulance became somewhat flustered and was having difficulty trying to insert an IV in her arm. He kept poking her with a needle and digging around for a vein. The discomfort from being repeatedly stuck bugged her. *Dude!* she thought. *You're messing with the only part of me that hasn't been shot, and it hurts!*

By the time she was brought into the emergency room at Orlando Regional Medical Center (ORMC), Fulford felt like she had been run over by a truck. Every part of her body hurt. She had been shot seven times. Jenkins's rounds had caught her in the right forearm, right shoulder, and left pinkie finger. Dzibinski's shots had hit her right knee, left ankle, left thigh, and left buttock. Ironically, even though she was wearing a bulletproof vest, it was never struck. One bullet went through the sleeve of her uniform, another hit her Taser, and a third destroyed her shoulder mic.

Fulford received stitches for several of her wounds and was released two days later. She didn't suffer any serious injury other than nerve damage in her right arm, which took months to heal. Martin was shot once in the left shoulder. He was also taken to ORMC, treated, and released a day later.

When Fulford was in the ER, the first thing she did was ask about the children. She felt extremely relieved to learn that, incredibly, the kids were unharmed despite being locked in a minivan that was being riddled with bullets. The SWAT team had to break out the windows to reach the children because the eight-year-old boy was too traumatized to open the doors—even for the police.

Among the first persons to arrive at the hospital to check on Fulford's condition were her mother, a former investigator for the state attorney's office; two sergeants; and Sheriff Kevin Beary. As Fulford was getting bandaged, she told Beary, "Call the training instructors and tell them thank you."

"What are you talking about?" the sheriff asked.

"Everything they taught me about tactics and a survival mind-set came to me when I most needed it," she replied. "I didn't have to think about anything that I did today. I automatically did it. That training helped save my life." Referring to the mandatory 32 hours of scenario-based training that deputies are required to take every year, she added, "I will never complain about having to do training again."

Later, she told her comrades, "When I think about what could have happened—how the children could have been injured or killed by those criminals—I am okay with what actually happened. If I hadn't tried to get the kids out and those bad guys had put the garage door down and harmed or killed them, I would always question myself. I did what I had to do.

"The gunmen could have run out the back door or given themselves up. They chose the way it ended because they came out shooting. I was just responding to the bad decision they made."

Investigators quickly pieced together the chilling facts of the crime.

John Dzibinski, a known felon with a warrant out for his arrest as a suspect in an earlier home invasion in North Charleston, South Carolina, had been tipped off to a large amount of marijuana and cash stashed inside the Pine Hills, Florida, home of Clinton and Isola Allen. The source said it would be an "easy score" because Clinton, a commercial painter, was out of town, leaving only his wife and three children at home. Dzibinski drove a burgundy Honda Passport SUV to the Orlando suburb with his friends George Jenkins, who had an extensive criminal record and was also named in the warrant, and Shaun Byrom, 20.

Early on the morning of May 5, Isola loaded the children in her minivan, planning to take the eight-year-old boy to school. She was backing out of the garage when the three men pulled into the driveway, blocking her path. One of them got out and, at gunpoint, ordered her to move over. Then he drove the vehicle back into the garage. The trio forced her into the house. Left alone in the minivan with his two-year-old twin sisters, the boy reached into his mother's purse, pulled out her cell phone, and called 911.

The three bad guys began loading their SUV in the driveway with garbage bags of marijuana, but happened to be inside the house when deputies arrived. Jenkins ordered Isola to get rid of the cops. When she couldn't persuade the deputies to leave, Dzibinski and Jenkins decided to shoot their way out, but ended up getting shot themselves. Jenkins was pronounced dead at the scene. Dzibinski was transported to the hospital where he was declared brain-dead and, a week later, taken off life support and died. Byrom, who had remained in the house and didn't fire his weapon, eventually surrendered. He was later tried and convicted of robbery and home invasion and sentenced to life in prison.

After deputies found 341 pounds of marijuana and more than $54,000 in cash at the couple's home, the Allens were charged with drug trafficking. Isola, 32, pleaded guilty and was sentenced to two months in jail and two years of community control followed by 10 years' probation. She was allowed to keep custody of the children. Clinton, 40, pleaded guilty and was sentenced to five years in prison.

"The eight-year-old boy was pretty remarkable," Fulford recalls. "He was a straight-A student who never missed school. He lived in a house with parents who were drug dealers who endangered him and his siblings by having all this marijuana and money in the home. He had the presence of mind to call 911. He did the right thing, even though he was living in that kind of environment. I want to believe that I saved those children so that when they grow up, they can do good things." She adds that she never heard from the family, not even a thank-you card.

Fulford returned to light duty 10 weeks after the gunfight and was back on full duty by the end of August. The following month, she exchanged wedding vows with a firefighter.

Fulford was promoted to detective in the child-abuse division, where she remained for three years before advancing to corporal and working with the patrol division. Following another promotion, this time to sergeant, she now heads up the department's driver-training facilities. As for her training in weak-hand shooting, it has really paid off for the right-hander. "I actually fire better now left-handed," she says.

For her courageous actions, Fulford received nearly a dozen major honors, including being named Deputy Sheriff of the Year by the National Sheriffs' Association and the 2005 Police Officer of the Year by the International Association of Chiefs of Police with a cover story about her heroics in the weekly magazine Parade. She also was the first woman awarded the Bureau of Justice's Public Safety Officer Medal of Valor, the highest national award for bravery given to a law enforcement officer, firefighter, or other emergency first responder.

Fulford received an enormous amount of positive feedback from women in law enforcement agencies throughout the country, mostly through letters, cards, and e-mails. She recalls, "The messages were pretty much the same: 'You don't know how much you've helped woman LEOs [law enforcement officers]. There is still a perception that we're not as good as the guys, that we're not as tough.' Well, the truth is, we are as tough."

DILEMMA IN A DEADLOCK

SENIOR CORPORAL BLAKE WILSON
Arkansas State Police

T he grueling day just wouldn't end. For hours and hours, Blake Wilson, a veteran of the Arkansas State Police's crisis negotiation team, had been standing in the blazing sun, trying to persuade an unstable, knife-wielding hostage taker to surrender and release his captives. But so far, the nail-biting dilemma remained at a deadlock.

Wilson knew that one wrong word, one false move on his part, could lead to the captives' injury or death. *That simply can't happen,* he vowed to himself.

Earlier that morning, October 31, 2007, Van Buren County Sheriff Scott Bradley had called the Arkansas State Police for assistance. The sheriff said a man was holding a mother and child at knifepoint in a truck in the parking lot of the US post office in the tiny community of Choctaw, about 65 miles north of Little Rock.

Wilson arrived on scene shortly after 8:00 a.m. and was briefed by Bradley. The sheriff said that the previous night, the suspect, Jeffrey Pearson, 30, while on drugs, had kidnapped his ex-wife and their four-year-old daughter, Abby, and spirited them away in his 1999 Dodge pickup. After family members alerted police to the abductions, officers searched the area. At 4:00 a.m., in the post office parking lot, a deputy found Pearson and his two hostages in the locked cab of his truck.

Pressing a knife against Abby's ribs, Pearson said he would speak only to his brothers, Jerry and Joe Pearson, and a former high school buddy, Josh Patterson, a police officer from the nearby town of Damascus. After the brothers and cop arrived, they talked to him through the driver's window, which was lowered only a few inches. Pearson said he was an emotional wreck because his girlfriend, Kim Parish, 26, had dumped him three weeks earlier and would have nothing more to do with him. Now he was demanding—under threat of harming Abby—that someone bring Kim to him so he could talk to her. He refused to surrender or release his hostages until Kim arrived.

At the end of the briefing, the sheriff told Wilson, "I want you to go talk to him."

A deputy had already brought Kim to the parking lot but, at Wilson's request, was kept out of Pearson's sight. She told Wilson that she would help police any way she could. Officers began conducting interviews with Pearson's family, friends, and coworkers, trying to learn as much as possible about the suspect.

"It's important to know all I can about him," Wilson told the sheriff. "What makes this guy tick? What's his endgame? What's important to him? What do I not say to him that will otherwise make him more agitated than he already is?"

Pearson was no stranger to police. In a 1997 court appearance, he had pleaded guilty to arson, burglary, and theft in Van Buren County. The judge had given him five years' probation without jail time. Pearson, a short, slightly built, bespectacled heavy-equipment operator, had stayed out of trouble since— until now.

Although the 50-year-old Wilson had never dealt with a situation quite like this, he felt confident that his years of experience as well as the 300 hours of hostage training he had received from FBI and military instructors would help him put an end to the tense conflict. *It shouldn't take more than an hour to get this resolved,* he thought.

Wilson strolled to the truck's passenger side where the window was rolled down. When he peered inside, he saw Abby on Pearson's lap, her back against his chest as she faced the steering wheel. Pearson was gripping a folding hunting knife in his left hand and keeping it pressed against her left side slightly above her waist. His ex-wife, a teacher's aide who had divorced him six months earlier, was in the center of the seat holding their daughter's right hand.

"Hello, Jeff," said the trooper in a friendly voice. "I'm Corporal Blake Wilson of the Arkansas State Police. I'm here to help you. So tell me, what's going on?"

"My girlfriend, Kim, has refused to talk to me for the last couple of weeks," Pearson complained. "Whenever I call, she hangs up on me. The last time I saw her, she spit in my face. I found out she's dating her old boyfriend, who just got out of prison. I must see her, and this is the only way I can get her to talk to me."

"Jeff, please release Abby," Wilson said. After Pearson shook his head, the trooper told him, "Listen to me, Jeff. This has nothing to do with your little girl. This is an adult problem. Let her go."

"No one is getting out of my truck until I talk to Kim."

"I can arrange for her to speak with you, but you have to give me your knife and release Abby and her mother first."

Several times Pearson agreed to drop the knife out the window but then went back on his word, prompting Wilson to think, *This is going to take longer than I thought.*

For the next few hours, Pearson seesawed emotionally, talking normally with Wilson one moment and becoming agitated the next. Still on drugs, he often mumbled to himself and bickered with his ex-wife, who was trying to talk sense into him. Abby mostly stayed quiet. Trying to prevent Pearson from doing anything rash, Wilson calmly maintained a constant dialogue with him.

"Why are you holding the people you love hostage?" Wilson asked.

"I'm doing this to get back at Kim," Pearson replied. "Any blood shed will be on her hands."

"What do you mean by that?"

"If I kill my family, then the police will be forced to kill me. Kim will have to live with that forever."

Hearing that chilling remark, Wilson thought, *He has such a warped mind he wants to kill his ex-wife and daughter and put the blame on his ex-girlfriend: "See what you made me do? It's all your fault." So that's his plan—to have all of them die and put Kim on a guilt trip.*

"You really don't want to do that," said Wilson. "Abby is your daughter, your own flesh and blood." Gazing at Abby, the trooper asked her, "When is your birthday, honey?" After she answered him, Wilson told Pearson, "Don't you want to see your daughter at her next birthday?"

Before Pearson could respond, Abby looked at Wilson and said, "Well, he didn't come to my last birthday."

Hoping her comment didn't anger Pearson, the trooper told her, "Maybe he was just too busy at work."

Earlier in the day, Wilson didn't believe Pearson would actually want to harm anyone. But when Pearson kept repeating his threats with growing conviction, the trooper began to fear the distressed hostage taker would try to carry them out. *A lot of times, people say stuff they don't mean, but he's beginning to sound like he means it. He's not worried about going to prison because he's planning on committing suicide by cop.* Wilson figured Pearson didn't have the gumption to kill himself and instead wanted to force the police to shoot him once he attempted to harm Abby or his ex-wife.

"It will all be over soon," Pearson muttered ominously.

Feeling a growing sense of urgency, Wilson kept talking and asking questions, trying to distract Pearson from the ugly thoughts percolating in his head. "You don't want to end your life like this," the trooper told him. "You don't want to be known in the community as the guy who killed his daughter. It will leave a stigma on your name forever. What would your family think about this?"

Pearson's knife hand began to twitch, and his brown eyes were fixed straight ahead at nothing.

He's getting agitated and restless, Wilson thought. *I need to get his mind off doing something bad.* "Jeff," he said. "Look at me, please."

Pearson turned his head and faced the trooper, who then asked, "What do you do for a living?"

"I operate heavy equipment, mostly a bulldozer," Pearson replied.

"Man," said Wilson, "I've always wanted to operate a 'dozer. I bet you feel like you're on top of the world when you're sitting on one of those things."

Pearson nodded. His sinister expression began to fade as he talked about how much he liked operating a bulldozer. For the next 45 minutes, the two discussed heavy equipment. Wilson kept up a steady stream of questions, which Pearson readily answered. Although he was acting less disturbed now, he still wouldn't give up the knife or his captives.

By noon, everyone in the truck was weary and thirsty, especially Abby. At Wilson's suggestion, which Pearson agreed to, the sheriff brought the girl a box of McDonald's chicken nuggets and a Dr Pepper. Abby drank the soda but didn't eat anything. She then fell asleep.

"You drugged Abby," Pearson accused Wilson. "You spiked the Dr Pepper hoping I would drink some of it and pass out."

"That's not true," the trooper replied. "Abby is exhausted because you've kept her up all night and half the day."

By now, many of the 50 members of the Arkansas State Police's SWAT and crisis negotiation teams had arrived and were deployed inside the post office and around the parking lot. Occasionally, Wilson would leave his spot by the truck and consult briefly with other officers and receive new information that police had gathered about Pearson.

Hoping Joe and Jerry Pearson could get through to their troubled brother, the trooper told them, "We don't want to hurt him. We want to end this peacefully. All he has to do is put the knife down and exit the vehicle. He will be taken into custody and have his day in court."

After the brothers talked to him again, Pearson seemed to weaken. He told Wilson, "I'll put down the knife if I can talk to Kim."

"Roll down your window and drop the knife on the ground," Wilson said. "Once you do that, we'll bring Kim around to the passenger-side window so you can talk to her."

"Is she even here?" Pearson asked.

On Wilson's instructions, officers escorted Kim to a spot far from the truck but in view of Pearson, who started to cry the moment he saw her. However, Pearson refused to toss out the knife, so Wilson ordered the police to move Kim out of sight.

The tension was mounting. So, too, was the discomfort level inside the truck caused by the unseasonably warm temperatures and the smell of urine after all three had wet themselves.

About 2:00 p.m., Pearson pressed the knife against Abby's chest. The little girl winced.

Alarmed, Wilson ordered, "Jeff, pull the knife away. I know you love your daughter and deep down you don't want to hurt her."

Abby turned her head, looked up at Pearson, and said, "Daddy, I don't know why you're doin' this to me, 'cause you're not supposed to hurt people you love."

She's a very impressive little girl, Wilson thought. *She has a good grasp on life for her age. Very mature. There's no way I'll let anything happen to her.*

Wilson tried numerous times to reason with Pearson about how he was treating his daughter, but the man showed no compassion. "Can you at least let Abby sit on her mother's lap?" the trooper asked.

Pearson shook his head and said, "I'm keeping her in my lap because you have snipers ready to kill me."

He's using her as a shield, Wilson thought. Even if snipers were in position—which they weren't—they wouldn't have been able to see their target through the truck's tinted windows. However, the SWAT team was preparing for a risky assault if necessary.

Throughout the day, Wilson was using body language, eye contact, and hand gestures to provide nonverbal information to the surrounding officers, which helped them plan for different possibilities. The trooper cleverly gave his comrades strategic information without raising Pearson's suspicions.

Once, when Pearson began acting irrationally again, the SWAT team was seconds away from launching its action plan of deadly force, but stood down after Wilson defused the strained moment. Pearson continued his emotional pattern of being relatively calm for short periods and then becoming unhinged.

"Jeff, you don't want to die, do you?" Wilson asked. When Pearson didn't respond, the trooper asked him, "Is your relationship with Kim worth your daughter's life?"

Pearson nodded and began crying. Then he started clenching his jaw, taking deep breaths, and staring out the windshield. With his arms wrapped around his daughter, he clutched the knife with both hands, resting the tip against Abby's chest. When she began to whimper, he said softly, "Don't worry. It will all be over soon."

My God, he's trying to work up the nerve to stab her! Wilson thought. *I'm going to have to shoot him.*

Wilson swiftly removed his gun from its holster and held it by his leg without Pearson seeing it. The trooper knew the next few critical seconds would determine whether he would shoot to save Abby's life. He didn't want to kill Pearson, especially with his daughter sitting on his lap. Besides, her mother was between Wilson and Pearson. From Wilson's position outside the passenger-side door, he didn't believe he had a clean shot. *But I'll shoot if I must.*

With his hand on the grip of his weapon, Wilson told himself, *I need to get his attention. I need him to make eye contact with me.* "Jeff!" Wilson barked. "Look at me! Look at me!" When Pearson turned toward the trooper, Wilson said, "Stop hurting Abby!"

Talking fast and furiously and with nerves on edge, Wilson coaxed Pearson into regaining control of himself. Once the immediate threat had passed, the trooper slipped his gun back into its holster. But he was worried. *Jeff is becoming more and more unstable.*

Wilson knew if he or the SWAT team had to rush in, they could save precious seconds with the doors unlocked. While Pearson was talking to his brother Jerry through the crack in the open driver-side window, Wilson reached through the open passenger window and pressed the automatic unlock button on the door's armrest. But Pearson heard the click and growled, "If you open that door, Abby's blood will be on your hands. Now lock the doors." Wilson did as he was told. The trooper later tried again to unlock all the doors, but Pearson locked them, this time without comment.

Two more hours passed without any progress. "Please release us," Abby's mother begged Pearson. "We both need to go to the bathroom."

"You can go, but Abby stays here with me," Pearson said.

If the mom gets out, that will give me a better shot at him, Wilson told himself.

"I will not leave Abby alone with you, Jeff," she declared.

Darn it, Wilson thought. *But I understand. If I were in her shoes, I wouldn't leave my daughter alone, either.*

As the stress ratcheted up again, Wilson suggested, "Let's all take a break to gather our thoughts." He had been on his feet since the morning without anything to eat or drink, yet surprisingly he wasn't hungry or thirsty. He was still too focused on his sole goal—ending this hostage crisis without anyone getting hurt.

The trooper walked away and consulted with members of his crisis negotiation team and SWAT team leader, Sergeant Bryan Davis. He and Davis were longtime friends who had started their careers with the Arkansas State Police as radio dispatchers. They decided that Davis should go back out with Wilson to offer tactical support. Because Pearson had said earlier he didn't want to see anyone in black SWAT uniforms, Davis donned jeans and a jacket.

Davis followed Wilson to the passenger side of the pickup. After Wilson introduced Davis, Pearson snapped, "I don't want him here." Miffed by the number of officers within 30 feet of the truck, he told Wilson, "In fact, I want everyone to move back, except for my brothers, Patterson, and you."

While the others stepped away, Wilson turned to Davis and said, "Go ahead and leave, too."

Davis walked toward the back of the truck and then quickly ducked down by the right rear wheel well. Pearson didn't notice because Wilson was blocking the side view mirror. Then Davis waddled closer to Wilson.

"Hey, where's the guy you introduced me to?" Pearson asked Wilson.

"He joined the others," Wilson lied.

"Well, I think there's still someone crawling around my truck."

"No, there isn't."

"I don't believe you," hissed Pearson. "Joe," he said to his brother, who was standing outside the driver's window. "Walk around the truck and see if there are any cops hiding from me."

Joe circled the pickup. Even though he could plainly see Davis, he told Pearson, "Nope. Nobody is hiding by your truck."

"Let me see for myself," Pearson said. To Wilson, he ordered, "Open the door."

What a break! Wilson had wanted to get the passenger door open all day. As he opened it, he stealthily pressed the button that unlocked all the doors—this time without Pearson realizing it. Wilson left the passenger door open. Now he gained a tactical advantage because he also positioned himself closer to Mrs. Pearson, which meant he was closer to the knife. *I might have to make a grab for it the first chance I get.*

"Let's just keep this door open so that no one can sneak up on you without your being able to see him," suggested Wilson, who was only inches away from the passenger seat.

While Wilson kept the conversation going by asking mundane questions about everyday life, he noticed that Pearson was getting sleepy. Pearson had been up for more than 24 hours, and the drugs that had been keeping him awake were wearing off. It was warm in the truck, and Wilson noticed that Pearson's head was starting to bob from drowsiness. *Maybe I can get the knife when he falls asleep.*

But Pearson didn't nod off. At about 5:00 p.m.—13 hours after he was first discovered with his two hostages by police— he once again agreed to put down the knife in exchange for a chance to talk to Kim. At the time, Pearson's brother Joe was standing with Officer Patterson near the driver's door. "Pass the knife to Joe, and I'll let Kim walk over to the truck," Wilson promised.

Pearson raised the knife toward the window. Joe placed his fingers through the small opening to receive it. But suddenly Pearson brought the knife back to Abby's chest. "How do I know Kim is still here?" he asked Wilson. "How do I know she'll even talk to me?"

"She's been here all day, Jeff," the trooper replied. "If she didn't care about you, she wouldn't have stayed. I'll show you."

Wilson arranged for police to escort Kim to a spot about 75 feet from the pickup where Pearson could see her. "I've kept my side of the bargain," said Wilson. "Now keep yours."

Pearson waved and blew kisses to Kim. She didn't respond. Despite Wilson's repeated demands to give up the knife, Pearson refused, so the trooper motioned the officers to take her away. Pearson began crying.

"I have an idea," his ex-wife told him. "If you give up the knife, I'll leave the truck and bring Kim back to you. Then you release Abby. Once that's done, Kim can come into the truck so you two can talk."

Pearson seemed willing to consider the plan. "That sounds like a good idea," Wilson told them. "We're going to let her get Kim for you, okay, Jeff?" *The moment he gives up the knife, we're rushing in there and taking him into custody.*

To Mrs. Pearson's right were a large purse, two jackets, a McDonald's bag, and a bottle of orange juice—items that would get in Wilson's way when he made his move. "Jeff, I'm going to remove these things to make it easier for her to get out, okay?" One at a time, Wilson placed the items from the passenger seat onto the hood of the truck.

But, like so many times before, Pearson backed out of the deal. He kept the knife pointed at Abby's chest.

I can't let this go on much longer, Wilson thought. *It'll be dark soon. He's never going to give up that knife, so I'm going to have to take it away from him. I just have to wait for the right opportunity.*

Although Mrs. Pearson was somewhat in his way, Wilson figured that with his five-foot ten-inch, 175-pound frame, he had enough space to burst past her and snare the knife. *I don't know if my plan will work, but I have to try—and I have to do it without Abby getting hurt.*

He noticed that Pearson was holding the knife with his left hand for a while and then switching it to his right hand. Wilson knew the best chance he had to grab the knife would be when Pearson held it in his right hand, closest to the trooper. Pearson also had to be looking the other way.

When Pearson was talking to his brother Joe, Wilson glanced down at Davis, who had remained crouched on the ground next to the pickup for more than two hours. Using hand gestures, the trooper indicated that he would try to overpower Pearson and gain control of the knife.

Davis shook his head and mouthed, "No, no, no."

Even though Davis outranked him, Wilson signaled, "It'll be okay."

Davis nodded and mouthed, "Be careful." Then he quietly pulled out a Taser gun, indicating that he would follow Wilson into the truck.

Like a runner at the starting blocks of a track meet, Wilson was poised to spring into action. Pearson held the knife in his right hand against Abby's chest. *Okay, Jeff, just look to your left,* Wilson wished. The trooper's muscles tensed up as he waited for the right moment to vault into the cab. Five minutes passed.

Pearson switched the knife to his left hand. *Darn it!* Wilson's body relaxed, but only slightly.

Pearson glanced briefly to his left. Then he switched the knife back to his right hand. *Get ready, get ready,* Wilson told himself, gearing up his body. Another five minutes passed. *Come on, Jeff, turn your head away.* Two minutes later, Pearson moved the knife to his left hand again. Three minutes later, he put it back in his right hand.

Yes! Now look left. Wilson's eyes were zeroed in on Pearson's head, waiting, waiting, waiting for him to turn away. Then it happened. One of the brothers approached the driver's side, distracting Pearson for just a second. With the swiftness of a leopard pouncing on its prey, Wilson lunged across Mrs. Pearson's lap and grasped Pearson's right wrist with both hands, shoving the knife away from Abby. Everyone in the cab screamed.

As Pearson and Wilson struggled for control of the weapon, Davis leaped into the truck, shoved Mrs. Pearson forward, climbed over her back, and drove his Taser into Pearson's neck. The strong electrical shock temporarily disabled Pearson, but it also sent a shock through Wilson's body because his hands were still wrapped around Pearson's wrist. The knife fell to the floor.

Pearson frantically fumbled with the door handle, trying to escape. But the SWAT team moved too quickly for him. A muscular six-foot four-inch trooper swung open the driver's door, snatched him with one hand, pushed him onto the pavement, and cuffed him. During the takedown, Abby tumbled to the ground but was unhurt.

And just like that, the hostage crisis was over.

For 10 grueling hours, Wilson had stood in the sun without food or water. He had tried everything in his arsenal—coaxing, sweet-talking, bargaining, reasoning, arguing—to make the hostage taker surrender and release his victims. Nothing worked, and yet everything worked. Because in the end, no one was killed; no one was injured. And the perpetrator was in custody.

Despite all the tension-filled, high-stakes hours Wilson endured, he didn't feel physically exhausted or mentally drained. He was actually feeling pretty good—great, in fact. As he strode from the crime scene, the trooper thought, *I feel like the quarterback who just threw the pass that won the big game.*

As Abby was escorted away from the pickup, she was smiling and waving at worried family members who had been standing behind police barricades. The first thing she did was hurry into the nearest bathroom. When she came out, she ran straight into an uncle's arms and hugged his neck.

Later at the police station, Wilson told her, "You were a brave little girl. I'm sorry this happened, but I'm sure your daddy loves you. It's just that he needs help. He's not thinking straight because he's on drugs."

Three days after the incident, her mother told Wilson that the little girl had a few bad nights right afterward but was otherwise doing fine. Mrs. Pearson also expressed to him her deep gratitude for ending the hostage crisis safely.

Wilson allowed Kim Parish to talk briefly with Pearson after his arrest. Pearson, who was charged with 10 felonies, was tried and convicted of two counts of kidnapping along with several lesser charges, including aggravated assault. He was sentenced to 34 years in prison and is currently serving time at the Arkansas Department of Correction in Cummins, Arkansas. He is eligible for parole in 2031.

For his tenacious role throughout the volatile incident, Wilson was named the 2007 Arkansas State Trooper of the Year and awarded the prestigious Medal of Valor. The Arkansas State Police also presented Davis with the highly regarded Trooper's Cross. He was later promoted to captain.

In a letter recommending the awards, Sergeant Jeff Crow, a SWAT team leader who had been on scene, wrote, "There is no doubt that the actions of Corporal Wilson and Sergeant Davis saved the life of the child and her mother. In addition to the brave and selfless act performed by Corporal Wilson . . . his professional and calm demeanor in the way he communicated with the suspect kept this situation from spiraling into a violent tragedy. The actions of Corporal Wilson and Sergeant Davis during this incident were perhaps the most valorous I have witnessed in my 22-year law enforcement career."

Both troopers also received national recognition. In Washington, DC, the National Law Enforcement Officers Memorial Fund named Wilson and Davis its Officers of the Month. In addition, the American Association of State Troopers voted Wilson the nation's 2008 Trooper of the Year.

"It's nice to receive the accolades," says Wilson, "but it was truly a team effort. Everyone there that day did their part so I could do mine."

His heroic effort impressed his proud wife, Sherry, in more ways than one. Recalls Wilson, "When I told her what happened, she said, 'You stood there for 10 hours and didn't have to go to the bathroom once?'"

After 37 years with the Arkansas State Police, including 13 years on its crisis negotiation team (3 of which as the team's commander), Wilson retired from his job on the last day of 2014. The following day, he started a new position as chief deputy of the Pope County Sheriff's Office in his hometown of Russellville, Arkansas. It was there, as a member of the third generation of his family to be born and raised in the town, where Blake Wilson had grown up dreaming of one day becoming a state trooper.

RESCUE OF
THE RESCUERS

DEPUTY TERRY BROWN,
SEARCH & RESCUE SWIMMER LOGAN
COUCH, AND LIEUTENANT JOHN WARD
Curry County Sheriff's Office (Oregon)

Harris Beach State Park, on the southern coast of Oregon, attracts campers, bird-watchers, and photographers with its spectacular ocean scenery and dramatic rocks. It beckons adventurous souls willing to brave its bone-chilling waters for bodysurfing in the breakers and skimboarding off the beach.

But for all its breathtaking beauty, the sea in these parts possesses a dark and dangerous trait: It sometimes lures unsuspecting visitors to their deaths.

Sneaker waves—they're called that because they're unpredictable and can appear without warning—often surge high up on the beach with tremendous force, sweeping you off your feet and dragging you into deeper water. They also carry heaps of heavy sand that can fill your clothes and weigh you down, increasing your chances of drowning. Lurking under the surface, powerful, crisscrossing rip currents can seize you and, no matter how good a swimmer you are, tow you out to sea.

Even if you are still alive after a sneaker wave or rip current hauls you away, you face another hazard—hypothermia, a critical loss of body heat. You have less than an hour to get rescued or you'll likely lose consciousness and drown in the cold water.

All these deadly elements came into play on June 2, 2014, when, during a courageous attempt to save a teenager, rescuers themselves needed rescuing.

In the early evening, 14-year-old Joshua Peterson, of Brookings, Oregon, was standing in knee-deep water with friends at windy Harris Beach. Unexpectedly, a sneaker wave hit him from behind and knocked him off his feet. As Josh struggled to regain his footing, a second wave pushed him down again. Before he could stand up, a forceful undertow yanked him away from the beach.

When he was only 15 feet from shore, he could no longer touch bottom or swim against the strong current, which was carrying him farther out toward heavy 10- to 15-foot breakers. Petrified, Josh screamed for help to his friends back on the beach. Unable to free himself from the current's grip, Josh felt his terror level rise by the minute.

At 5:38 p.m., Deputy Terry Brown, 33, was in Brookings two miles away when dispatch alerted him to a boy caught in the treacherous currents off Harris Beach. Four minutes later, Brown arrived at the parking lot, which sat 200 feet above the beach. From his vantage point, he saw Josh struggling to stay afloat offshore. Brown noticed there was no one on the beach who could do anything for the lanky youth because they had no equipment, not even a long rope. He also knew it would take time for search-and-rescue volunteers to arrive because they didn't have emergency vehicles.

Dispatch reported that other first responders were heading to the scene and that the Coast Guard was launching a 25-foot vessel known as a SAFE boat from its Chetco River station four miles away. But Brown was worried the boy wouldn't last long enough for the Coasties to rescue him because he had been treading water for nearly 15 minutes—about the time for the onset of hypothermia.

I have to act fast, Brown thought. *But it shouldn't be that big of a deal. I'll go out, grab the kid by the scruff of the neck, and bring him safely back to the beach. I'll TCB [take care of business] quickly.*

Brown grabbed a life vest and a backpack that could unfurl an attached 100-foot-long lifeline—items that he always kept in the trunk of his squad car. He raced down to the beach, took off his duty belt, shoes, socks, and uniform shirt, and donned the life vest and backpack. Giving one end of the rope to fellow deputy Joel Hensley, Brown said, "Hold on to this. When I reach him, pull us back in."

When Brown plunged into the 52-degree water, his body was shocked by the cold. But after the initial jolt to the system, he paid little attention to the discomfort because his adrenaline was flowing and his mind was concentrating on saving Josh. The hardest part for Brown was getting past the breakers that were churning just offshore. Twice they struck him down. He expended so much energy fighting through them that once he succeeded and started swimming, he was already getting tired. But the current that had pulled Josh out was also the one that carried the deputy toward the teenager.

Brown wasn't even halfway to Josh when the deputy felt a tug on his back. *Oh, no*, he thought. *I've run out of rope. The boy is a lot farther out than I thought, at least another 200 feet away from me.* The taut lifeline was holding Brown back, so he whipped off the backpack, which was still attached to the rope, and continued swimming. He no longer could hear what anyone on the beach was yelling at him because of the noise of the wind and crashing waves. He also had water in his ears.

By the time Brown neared Josh, the deputy was breathing heavily from exertion. He deliberately stopped about 10 feet from Josh and talked to him to assess whether the boy would be panicky and hamper the rescue. Brown quickly determined that Josh was scared but holding himself together and doing a decent job of treading water.

"We're going to get you out of here," Brown pledged. "But I need you to stay calm."

"Yes, sir," replied Josh, shivering from the cold. "I will."

"The Coast Guard is coming, we have people onshore ready to help, and now I'm out here, so we're going to be fine, okay?"

"Yes, sir."

Brown swam over to Josh and held him, letting the deputy's life vest keep their heads above water. After telling each other their names, Brown said, "Let's float for a couple of minutes and catch our breath. We're going to make it, Josh. I promise you, we're going to make it. Let's buddy up and stay afloat to conserve our energy and body heat. Just hold on to me."

Grasping each other chest-to-chest was a cold-water survival technique that Brown had learned during his days as a Coastie. Following in the footsteps of his father and brother, Brown had joined the Coast Guard right out of high school. He left the service six years later after being diagnosed with Raynaud's, a chronic disease that causes parts of the body, especially fingers and toes, to go numb from cold.

With this condition, Brown couldn't have been in a worse situation, drifting in the frigid water. At six feet and 160 pounds, he had little body fat for insulation. Despite losing feeling in his fingers, he kept a firm hold on Josh. *There's no way I'm letting go of him*, the deputy told himself.

"Let's try swimming back to shore together, okay?" Brown said.

Still clutching each other, they flipped onto their backs and began kicking, hoping to break free of the current. But they weren't making any headway, even when they tried different strokes and positions. The only thing they were getting closer to was exhaustion. *Maybe this isn't the greatest idea I've ever had*, the deputy thought.

The wind was kicking up, and the five-foot swells were getting bigger. Every 15 to 20 seconds, another set of waves washed over them. "Try not to swallow too much seawater," Brown said.

The large rocks that extended out from the beach were creating menacing currents and erratic waves. When the breakers rolled in and crashed against the rocks, the water moved back out like a whirlpool, causing the currents to swirl around and carry the two in one direction and then another. At one point, the two of them were on the far north side of the beach, so close to shallow water that Brown's toes actually touched the sandy bottom. But before they could get any closer, the current shoved them straight back out and then pushed them southward.

Treading water, Brown kept Josh's head above the surface, occasionally yelling to police officers and firefighters who had climbed onto the nearby rocks that the two were okay for the moment, but desperately needing help. The men on the rocks weren't equipped to enter the cold water and reach them, so all they could do was shout encouragement to the pair.

Bobbing in the heavy swells, Brown and Josh soon spotted a boat. "The Coast Guard is here," the deputy said. "It should be only a few minutes before we're out of the water." They could see the boat briefly only when they rose to the top of a wave before the boat disappeared from view as they slid toward the bottom of the swell.

The waves were breaking so roughly between the pair and the boat that the vessel couldn't get any closer. Life preservers were tossed overboard for them, but Josh and Brown were too far away to reach them. Brown was getting frustrated. *Why isn't someone jumping in the water? They must realize by now that we can't make it to shore on our own. Nothing is happening. They should have had us out of the water by now.*

Then he saw the boat pull away. "The water is just too rough for the small boat," Brown told him. "They're probably going to return with their bigger one." The deputy was right. The Coast Guard had dispatched its 47-foot vessel, known as a motor lifeboat, in another effort to rescue them.

To take their minds off their grave predicament, Brown and Josh made small talk. They chatted about their families, the deputy's work, Josh's school, and life itself.

Having been in the water for 15 minutes, Brown could no longer ignore its perilously cold temperature. Symptoms of hypothermia were starting to show: chattering teeth, shivering body, loss of feeling in his hands and feet. He knew his body was consolidating the blood around his core to keep the lungs and heart as warm as possible, leading to muscle weakness and fatigue. And he knew what happens to victims when muscle weakness and fatigue take hold—they're unable to hold up their heads, and they pass out and drown.

It took all of Brown's strength and resolve to hold on to Josh, who was suffering similar symptoms, having been in the water even longer. Every minute that went by, Brown felt himself getting shakier. Having trouble keeping water out of his mouth from being hit by the waves, he was soon swallowing so much salt water that he began throwing up.

Brown's belief that the two would be rescued was beginning to weaken. *If the Coast Guard can't do anything to help us, then who can? I don't know what, if anything, the people onshore are doing. Are we going to make it?* But he didn't dare confide that fear to Josh.

He not only was on the edge of losing hope, he was also on the verge of losing something else—consciousness.

Sheriff's Lieutenant John Ward—a longtime search-and-rescue (SAR) veteran—was off-duty 25 miles away when dispatch radioed him: "There's a subject in the water and a deputy out with him, and they can't get back to shore. The deputy has been out there for fifteen minutes, and the boy for a half hour."

Why is the deputy out in the water? Ward wondered. *He wouldn't have a dry suit or a wet suit on, only a life jacket that all deputies carry in their cruisers. He doesn't have anything to fight off the cold water for an extended period of time. This is serious.*

As a SAR coordinator for the county for several years, Ward had extensive training in the surf and was involved in plenty of water rescues—as well as recoveries of dead victims. Having lived his entire life in the area, he had a healthy respect for the dangers of the coastal waters. He liked to remind people, "The ocean is unforgiving and doesn't care who you are."

How many times had the volunteer SAR team retrieved the body of a swimmer who was dragged out to sea by a riptide and drowned? How many times had the team been called on to help save a victim of hypothermia? How many times had the team rescued someone after a sneaker wave swept him off his feet and left him in the clutches of powerful currents exactly like this emergency? Too many, Ward knew.

"Send out the SAR white-water team," Ward told dispatch. "I'm on my way." After he jumped into his patrol rig, Ward called Logan Couch, his assistant SAR coordinator and said, "I've got a deputy and a boy in the water, and it looks bad. No one can reach them because of the currents. Can you help?"

Couch replied, "I'll be right there."

Forty-two-year-old Logan Couch had been a member of the volunteer SAR team for 10 years and had participated in many rescues and even more recoveries. As the co-owner of a small security business, he had been putting in long hours for weeks, and this day was no exception. Weary and looking forward to a relaxing evening, Couch had just arrived home—which was only a mile from the beach—when he received Ward's call. He hopped into his truck, which was loaded with rescue gear, and raced to the scene.

Arriving at the parking lot, Couch saw members of the Brookings Police Department and Fire Department huddled on the beach, and he spotted Brown floating on his back with Josh hanging on to him. Brown's head was pointed toward the beach and his feet pointed out to sea. Every time a wave rolled in, Josh climbed onto Brown's right shoulder, which pushed the deputy's head underwater. Couch thought, *Terry isn't able to fight off the waves. He's just floating there, taking it. It can only mean one thing—he's hypothermic.*

Couch grabbed his gear—a dry suit, helmet, and throw rope—and ran down the ramp and onto the beach, where he sprinted for about a quarter mile to the crowd that had gathered around the police and firefighters. Nobody had enough rope to reach the pair. He immediately put on his dry suit—insulated, waterproof outerwear—right over his street clothes. Unlike a wet suit that allows water to dribble in, a dry suit keeps water out and is more buoyant because it has air in it.

As Couch prepared to go after the pair, a police officer came over to him and said, "Stand down. The Coast Guard is on its way."

I don't think the Coast Guard can reach them, Couch thought. *This guy is a police officer. He doesn't have control over the sheriff's office, so I'm going to ignore his order.*

An onlooker rushed to a nearby campground and fetched a kayak. Although Couch didn't think it would help him, he gave it a try at the urging of others on the beach. He paddled the kayak into the crashing waves, only to capsize. He tried a second time, but once again the waves slapped him in the chest and tossed him out of the kayak.

Hurt, tired, and having difficulty breathing from the beating, the five-foot nine-inch, 180-pound rescue swimmer staggered ashore and abandoned the kayak. People were yelling for someone to do something to help the struggling pair. Then Couch heard one voice above all others. It was coming from inside his head, and it said simply, "Go!" He had no idea if it was a voice from the beyond or his own conscience or God.

Whatever the source, it bolstered him with a surge of confidence and strength. All anxiety, worry, and stress disappeared, replaced by a rock-solid conviction that he would bring Brown and Josh back to shore alive.

Couch plunged into the water and, by swimming furiously, busted through the first set of breakers. Like Brown, Couch was then whisked out by the strong current. When he reached the pair, it was obvious to him that Brown was faltering. The deputy was throwing up and moaning. Surprisingly, Josh, who had a slender build, didn't seem as badly affected by the cold, though he was shivering. Couch was relieved to see the boy was fairly calm under the dire circumstances.

"It's all right; it's all good," Couch told them. "Just relax, and we'll figure out a way to get back to shore."

His first priority was to relieve Brown of holding on to Josh so that the deputy didn't have to labor so much to keep his own head above water. Couch took over the responsibility of holding on to the boy and keeping everyone together.

Every time a wave washed over them, Josh tried to climb up on Couch's shoulder, which pushed Couch and Brown underwater. Several times, Couch had to shove Josh off him and remind the boy, "I will hold you. You don't hold me." Josh would always reply, "I'm sorry."

The Coast Guard returned with the bigger boat, but it couldn't get near the trio because the risk was too great that the hazardous waves would drive the vessel against the rocks or shove it aground in the shallow water. The boat finally backed away. There was nothing more the Coast Guard could do for them.

I knew they wouldn't be able to save us, Couch thought. *We should try swimming toward the beach even though we might not reach it. It's better than just treading water and waiting for someone else to try to rescue us. It gives us something to do.*

They began making some progress toward shore. But the current was toying with them, moving them in and out, left and right. It pushed them closer to the beach, and just when it seemed they could dig their heels into the sandy bottom of the shallower water, it jerked them right back out. To Couch, it felt like an invisible rope was tied around them and hooked to a pickup that pulled them away from any chance at a rescue.

Couch's dry suit had sprung a leak, and a great deal of water had poured into each leg. Weighed down, he was now floating more vertically than horizontally. The waves were picking the three of them up and dropping them hard, sometimes right onto the seabed. One wave shoved Couch so hard that when he hit a shallow section of the bottom, it wrenched his knee, leaving him in pain.

The current pushed them along the face of a house-sized rock. The waves rolled over them, hit the side of the rock, and then rebounded, striking them in the face. Shoving them forward and backward, the waves relentlessly pounded them from all directions.

At one point, Brookings police officer Kyle Kennedy took a rope and climbed onto the rocks, where he stripped off his duty belt and gun and waded out to reach the trio. Even though the waves were whacking him and the current was trying to knock him off his feet, Kennedy doggedly tried to snare them as they went by. When they were close enough—only 25 yards away from the beach—he tossed a lifeline. Couch grabbed it, but the current was so powerful it pulled the rope right out of Kennedy's hands, and they were carried out again. "I'm sorry!" Kennedy shouted. "I'm so sorry!" He almost drowned trying to work his way back to the rocks.

Brown's physical condition was worsening, and he started to go into convulsions, which scared Josh. "I know it looks bad," Couch told the boy, "but he'll survive. We all will. I promise." *It's tough for Josh to see someone who was trying to save him now be in such bad shape,* he thought. *At least Josh is doing pretty well.*

The current pushed them near another group of rocks, this time ones that were blocking the biggest waves. "We're in a better position here," he told Josh and Brown. "This is a good spot." Then he saw a man in a dry suit scrambling over the rocks. "We should be out of the water in just another few minutes," Couch said. "I see who's coming."

When Ward arrived at the beach, frustration was boiling over among the crowd of 30 onlookers and first responders. By the time he donned his dry suit, it had been about 50 minutes since Josh had been swept off the beach, about 35 minutes since Brown entered the water, and about 15 for Couch. *They are in serious trouble*, Ward thought. *They're running out of time.* He knew hypothermia was setting in.

Bringing along a 350-foot rope that he always carried in his patrol vehicle, Ward handed one end to the officers on the beach and told them, "Whatever you do, don't let go." Then he worked his way over the rocks, making sure the rope wouldn't get snagged on them.

When he climbed over a large rock, he saw that he was within range of the three. By now, Brown looked like he was barely conscious. His skin was white and his lips were blue.

I just hope I have enough rope to reach them, Ward thought. He wrapped the remainder of the rope around his arm and then jumped into the water. The 56-year-old, five-foot eight-inch, 165-pound lieutenant was in excellent physical shape and thought he could swim to them within a minute.

But to his dismay, cold water was leaking into his suit. It had ripped on jagged edges and prickly barnacles while he had crawled along the rocks. Weighed down by the seeping water, Ward found swimming much more difficult than he imagined because he was also fighting against the waves, wind, and currents. *I have to save them*, he told himself. *I can't let them die on my watch.*

Gagging from ingesting water in the heavy swells, Ward kept stroking his way toward them, ignoring the pain in his arms and legs. Progress was slow and difficult. *There are three people in the water*, he told himself. *They're counting on me. Well, I'm not going to fail.*

Watching Ward grapple with the elements, Couch

hollered, "Come on, John, let's go!" While holding Josh against his right shoulder and raised right knee, Couch had his left hand through the shoulder strap of Brown's life vest so the deputy couldn't float away.

Ward was within 75 feet of them, then 50 feet, then 25 feet. *Almost there!* When he was tantalizingly close—only 10 feet away—he felt a strong jerk against his arm. His heart sank because he knew what had happened.

"Logan, I've run out of rope!" he shouted to Couch. "I can't get any closer. You've got to swim my way. Battle with everything you've got!"

While holding on to Brown and Josh, Couch told the boy, "We have to kick, paddle, and swim toward the lieutenant."

Despite their valiant efforts to cut through the current, they couldn't close the distance between them and Ward, who had to remain where he was because he couldn't let go of the lifeline. They had to find a way to bridge that 10-foot gap.

Then it dawned on Couch: *We'll use Terry as our lifeline.* The deputy was floating on his back, his eyes closed, his body almost lifeless. Holding on to Brown's ankles, Couch shoved the deputy past him and Josh and toward Ward, hoping Ward could grab him. But when Couch pushed Brown as far as he could without letting go, Brown was still a few feet from Ward. "Terry! Put your arm behind your head!" Couch shouted. "Come on, Terry, you can do it."

Briefly regaining consciousness, Brown slowly raised his arm until it was over his head, where it wavered for a second before flopping down behind his head. Then he lost consciousness again.

Kicking furiously, Couch and Josh inched Brown closer to Ward, who stretched out until, finally, he touched the deputy's fingertips. After one more kicking burst from Couch and Josh, Ward clasped Brown's hand and shouted triumphantly, "I've got him!"

Drawing the three of them toward him, Ward tied the rope around them and himself. Then he gave the signal to the first responders at the other end of the lifeline to start pulling. After the initial tug toward shore, Ward felt a tremendous sense of relief, knowing that this crisis would soon end in a successful rescue.

After the four were reeled through the last of the breakers, the first responders waded into the surf and pulled the unconscious deputy out with Ward's help. They were so focused on Brown that they momentarily forgot about Josh. The next wave that came in knocked the boy over and pushed Couch on top of him.

The two stumbled out of the water. Couch glanced at Brown, whose skin was gray and lips were purple. The deputy wasn't moving at all. *Is he dead?* Couch wondered. *If he's not, he's really close to death.*

Ward bent over Brown and said, "Hang in there, Terry. Everything is going to be fine." But the deputy didn't respond.

Still shivering, Josh walked up to Ward, gave him a hug, and said, "Thanks for saving my life." Then he went over to Couch and did the same thing.

Harris Beach park rangers brought an all-terrain vehicle down to the beach to carry Brown and Josh to a waiting ambulance, which transported them to Sutter Coast Hospital in Crescent City, California, about 30 miles away.

As those two were being taken away, Couch and Ward remained on the beach, coughing up swallowed seawater.

"Are you all right, John?" Couch asked.

"I'm good," Ward replied. "And you?"

"Fine. Just fine."

Ward grinned and said, "We did it, Logan."

Couch nodded and patted him on the back. After gathering his gear, Couch headed up to the parking lot without saying another word to anyone. But he couldn't stop thinking about the SAR volunteer team's motto: "So others may live."

Brown arrived at the hospital in critical condition because his body temperature was 89 degrees, a sign that he was suffering from moderate to severe hypothermia. After being warmed up and treated with IV solutions, he made a rapid recovery and was released the next day. Josh was listed in stable condition from hypothermia. He, too, spent only one night in the hospital. The first thing he did the next morning was find Brown and personally thank him.

"I was really scared at first," Josh told reporters. "I was out there for about 20 minutes until Terry showed up. If he hadn't come out, I would have been a goner."

Ward, who took over as sheriff of Curry County four months later, recalls, "It was one of the most dramatic rescues we've had in the area. Josh would have definitely drowned had Terry not reached him. And if Logan hadn't gone out there, Josh and Terry would have drowned or succumbed to hypothermia. I just happened to be the one who went out and got the rope to them so we were all brought back in. This was a combined effort from everybody."

For their roles in saving Josh's life, Brown, Couch, and Ward received various honors.

The Carnegie Hero Fund Commission, which annually recognizes people who risked their lives trying to save others, presented Brown with its prestigious Carnegie Medal. The Oregon State Sheriffs' Association gave Brown its highest honor for bravery, the Award for Valor.

The United States Coast Guard also honored Brown with its Gold Lifesaving Medal, one of only two in the nation approved by the service in 2015. Couch was given the Silver Lifesaving Medal. Ward received the Certificate of Valor while Kennedy, of the Brookings Police Department, was presented with the Meritorious Public Service Award.

At the Coast Guard ceremony, Brown, who took a position as a sheriff's deputy in Polk County, Oregon, said, "We don't do this for the awards or recognition, because it's just what we do." But, he added, "It's nice to be appreciated."

Calling the rescue a true team effort, Couch says, "We have one another's back, and we always want to come home together. We'll do whatever it takes for this community because we believe in ourselves."

LIFE AND DEATH IN A SHOOT-OUT

SERGEANT NATE HUTCHINSON
Weber County (Utah) Sheriff's Office

Sergeant Nate Hutchinson charged into the house where he and five other officers had already been shot by a vicious gunman who was still concealed inside, lying in wait for anyone who dared enter.

Nothing was going to stop Hutchinson. It didn't matter that his weapon was out of ammunition. And it certainly didn't matter that he had taken a bullet in his right hip while rescuing a seriously wounded officer moments earlier. There was another fallen comrade inside who needed help, and Hutchinson was determined to pull him out, too.

Crossing into the kill zone, Hutchinson reached down to grab hold of his bullet-riddled buddy who was sprawled on the floor. Just then, Hutchinson was shot in the left arm and again in the left rib cage. Refusing to seek cover as bullets continued to whiz past him, Hutchinson began dragging his comrade away from the line of fire. Suddenly, out of the corner of his eye, he spotted the shadowy figure of the gunman emerging from a few feet away.

Staring at the assailant's weapon, Hutchinson thought, *Well, this is it. This is where I die.*

Hutchinson, then 35, of the Weber County Sheriff's Office, was a member of the Weber-Morgan Narcotics Strike Force, a group made up of law enforcement officers from Weber and Morgan Counties, including the Ogden Police Department, in Utah. It was dangerous work because the agents regularly encountered high-level armed criminals who dealt with large quantities of drugs and money. Working undercover, the officers wore regular clothes instead of uniforms, and many sported beards and long hair.

One day, a woman called the strike force, claiming her ex-boyfriend, Matthew David Stewart, 37, was operating a small grow house—using his residence to grow marijuana in his basement and selling it. Usually, the agents focused on hard-core dealers, but the law is the law, so they decided to investigate. If the tip turned out to be true, the cops thought that in exchange for leniency, Stewart might cooperate with them and provide information that could lead to busting a bigger drug operation.

What the woman failed to tell the agents was that Stewart, who had served in the military, was armed and had vowed to her, "If police ever come to my house, I'll shoot it out with them."

In the last week of December 2011, the strike force went on four separate occasions to Stewart's small two-bedroom, one-bath redbrick house on Jackson Avenue in Ogden, hoping to talk to him. But every time they knocked, no one came to the door, although there was always a light on in the kitchen.

Deciding they needed to get inside, the agents obtained a search warrant—a court order from a judge allowing them to enter the home and secure any evidence. On the evening of January 4, 2012, Hutchinson and eight of his colleagues arrived at the house for what they assumed would be a routine search. Even though they didn't expect any trouble, all nine members of the unit went because they anticipated collecting plenty of evidence and wanted to secure each room during the search. Besides, they didn't know who they might encounter. It hadn't been that long ago when they entered a grow house and discovered 32 people inside.

As a precaution, the agents wore bulletproof vests. Hutchinson, however, didn't have one because the straps on his body armor broke when he was putting it on. At the time, he thought, *Well, we're searching a little marijuana grow, so it's not a big deal.*

Although they were in plain clothes and jeans, they all wore badges as well as apparel, such as jackets and vests, that identified them as police officers. Hutchinson was in a vest that said WEBER-MORGAN POLICE on the back and a ball cap that said STRIKE FORCE POLICE.

The run-down split-level house had a narrow driveway and a carport. A side door led from the carport to a small landing in the home. From there, a set of stairs went down to the basement, and four steps went up to the kitchen on the main level.

While Hutchinson stood outside the front door, the others lined up by the side door. Jason Vanderwarf, the case agent, knocked and announced in a loud voice, "Police! Search warrant! Come to the door!" After no response, he knocked again and said, "Police. Search warrant." Still nothing. The house was so small that Hutchinson knew if Stewart was inside, he certainly would have heard them. After the third knock, agent Jared Francom used a battering ram to breach the door. The agents poured into the house, calling out, "Police! Search warrant! Come out!"

Hutchinson hopped off the front porch and was the last person to enter the house through the side door. He hustled down to the basement and saw that it had been transformed into a hydroponic grow room, where marijuana plants were being raised in tubes of water. The basement had its own special lighting and ventilation system to grow the weed.

While he was examining the setup, Hutchinson heard a burst of gunfire—five distinct shots—coming from the main level. Then silence. *Uh-oh, there must be a guard dog that went after the guys,* he thought. Often drug dealers will keep vicious trained dogs in a grow house to protect them from the police as well as from bad guys seeking to rob them of money or drugs.

But then Hutchinson heard yells and someone shout, "Out! Out!" *This isn't about a guard dog,* he thought. *Maybe the suspect shot at them and jumped out the window.* So the agent dashed up the stairs from the basement, out the side door, and into the backyard to look for the gunman. Not seeing or hearing anything outside, Hutchinson went into the house and up the steps to the kitchen area.

Just then, one of the agents, Shawn Grogan, of the Ogden Police Department, staggered around the corner, pressing his hands on both sides of his face, which was bleeding badly. A bullet had gone through one cheek and exited the other. Grogan crashed into the wall and began sliding down, but Hutchinson caught him before he could slump to the floor. Because of the injury, Grogan couldn't talk, but his wide eyes said it all: He was hurt and in shock.

Hutchinson realized there had been an exchange of gunfire. Not hearing anything else, he thought, *Maybe the suspect was shot.* Hutchinson put his arm around Grogan's waist and helped him out of the house and down the driveway. Meeting another agent, Hutchinson said, "Grogan is hurt. He's been shot. We don't have time to wait for an ambulance. Put him in one of our cars and drive him to the hospital. I'll stay here on scene and deal with whatever we're facing inside."

As Hutchinson sprinted back up the driveway, he heard another agent shout, "He's inside! He's inside!" Immediately, gunfire erupted again. Hutchinson pulled out his .40-caliber

Glock pistol and burst through the side door. He bounded up the steps and stopped for a brief moment, trying to determine where the shooting was coming from and where his comrades were. *Don't run into a bullet*, he told himself.

He saw two agents—Jared Francom and Kasey Burrell—by a half wall that separated the kitchen from the dining area. They were shooting down a darkened hallway that led to two bedrooms and a bathroom. From the doorway of one of the rooms, Matthew Stewart was firing his Beretta pistol. Because the light was on in the kitchen, but not in the hallway, it was easy for the gunman to see the two agents but difficult for them to see him.

Chaos reigned in the kitchen as bullets slammed into the walls, stove, cabinet, and refrigerator. Pieces of drywall and metal flew in all directions. The noise was deafening.

Hutchinson noticed the slide on Francom's semiautomatic pistol was in the back position. When that type of weapon is out of bullets, the slide automatically locks. "I'm out of ammo," Francom told Hutchinson.

But the house was so small that Stewart heard him, too, and let loose with a salvo of shots that dropped Francom and Burrell. They lay motionless on the floor. To Hutchinson, the agents were more than just comrades in arms. They were his good buddies.

I've got to get them out of here, Hutchinson told himself. But with an active shooter blasting away, the agent knew he was putting himself at grave risk.

Because Burrell was curled up on the floor, and the closest to the gunman, Hutchinson decided to try to retrieve him first. Gripping his Glock, which held 14 rounds in its magazine, Hutchinson began shooting down the hallway for covering fire as he jumped over Francom's body and moved toward Burrell, who had been shot in the head.

Bullets were zipping so close to Hutchinson that he could feel the movement in the air from their wake. It was like speeding on a motorcycle without a helmet through a swarm of bees. Only these weren't stinging insects; these were deadly projectiles. Although he didn't yell anything at the gunman, Hutchinson wanted to say, *Just stop shooting at us for a few seconds so I can get these guys out of the house.*

As he reached for Burrell, Hutchinson felt a bullet tear into his right front hip and lodge in his lower back. The impact felt like someone had struck him hard with a baseball bat. He let out a grunt from the initial pain and kept on firing until he ran out of ammunition. *Nothing more I can do about it. Stay focused on getting Kasey out of here.*

Sticking his gun in his waistband, Hutchinson began dragging Burrell away from the hallway and into the kitchen. When Stewart unleashed another barrage, Hutchinson ducked and then yanked his fellow agent down the steps to the landing and away from the gunfire. Burrell didn't move on his own, which made Hutchinson worry that he might be dead.

By now, the other officers who had been inside had retreated outside and formed a perimeter around the house, waiting to apprehend Stewart if he tried to escape. Meanwhile, one of the agents had radioed for more backup.

While officers moved Burrell to safety, Hutchinson thought, *If I go back inside, there's no way I'll make it out alive. I have no more ammo. But I can't leave Jared in there to die. He'd do the same for me. I've got to try. Either I get shot or I don't.*

At six feet, 240 pounds, Hutchinson made a large target. Ignoring the wound in his hip, he hobbled back into the house, up the steps, and into the kitchen, where he encountered more gunfire. As he bent over Francom, Hutchinson felt a second bullet strike him in the left bicep. The bullet drilled through his muscle, barely missing the bone, and exited out the back of his upper arm.

Gritting his teeth, he grabbed Francom. But then a third bullet hit Hutchinson, this time in the rib cage on his left side just below his armpit. Another bullet struck him, but luckily it was deflected by his badge, which was dangling from his waistband off his right hip.

Whatever pain he was feeling, it was overshadowed by his growing anger and frustration. In his mind, he told Stewart, *Give me a break and let me get him out of here. I'm not coming after you.*

Bleeding from his left arm, left rib cage, and right hip, Hutchinson put his hands under Francom's arms and began backpedaling while dragging him through the kitchen. But then the agent saw Stewart coming toward him. As the gunman took careful aim at him, Hutchinson braced himself for the next bullet, which he fully expected would kill him.

Realizing he was at the top of the steps, Hutchinson figured he had one chance to survive. He leaned back and, while still holding onto Francom, fell backward on the stairs. The bullet whooshed past Hutchinson's head by a hairbreadth. The two slid down the steps to the landing with Francom's limp, six-foot two-inch, 260-pound body resting on top of him.

Lying on his back and looking up the stairwell, Hutchinson saw Stewart's Beretta sticking out from a corner, then a hand, then an arm. Stewart didn't step out into the doorway, but he started blindly firing his weapon, moving his hand around, spraying the stairwell.

Bleeding from his three gunshot wounds and pinned under the dead weight of his heavy buddy, Hutchinson felt helpless. *I can't do anything.* Bullets were hitting the wall inches from his head, which was getting pelted by splinters of wood and drywall.

Hutchinson was alarmed by the ruthlessness of the gunman. From past experience and training, the agent knew that almost always, bad guys shoot to get away from the police. But not Stewart—he was super aggressive. He had come from a back bedroom and advanced down the hall, shooting Burrell and Francom and then firing at Hutchinson, who was only trying to pull his pals to safety.

Just when he was sure he would be killed in the next instant, Hutchinson heard a click. Oh, what a wonderful sound that was to him. *He's run out of bullets!* Stewart's hand pulled the gun back behind the corner of the room, giving Hutchinson time to roll Francom off him.

As he began to lug Francom out into the carport, Hutchinson thought, *Stewart's coming after us. He's going to follow me and Francom right out into the carport and continue shooting until he kills us. But how can I fight back? I have no bullets.*

Hutchinson looked down at the landing and, to his amazement, saw a shotgun lying on the floor. *Oh, wow! This could be my saving grace!*

He wasn't aware that minutes earlier, Officer Michael Rounkles of the Ogden Police Department had been only a block away in his squad car when he heard the radio message requesting backup in an officer-involved shooting (OIS). When the uniformed cop pulled up to the house, he heard gunfire inside, so he took his police-issued shotgun and ran up the driveway. He was followed by Vanderwarf.

While Hutchinson had been dragging Burrell into the kitchen, Rounkles and Vanderwarf had darted into the house and up the steps. Seconds later, Rounkles was shot. He dropped his shotgun, fell to the floor, and rolled down to the landing. Still conscious, he had the presence of mind to crawl out of the house and onto the driveway. The other officers outside carried him to the street, put him in a squad car, and rushed him to the hospital.

At the same moment that Rounkles was shot, another bullet had grazed Vanderwarf in the hip, knocking him down the stairs. He then had limped out of the house.

Now that the bloodied Hutchinson had found the shotgun, he picked it up and told himself, *I've got to at least make a stand and give my other guys time to get the wounded to safety.* He lurched up the steps and into the kitchen. Just then, Stewart jumped into the doorway so that the two were facing each other at no more than three feet apart.

"Aaaahhh!" the gunman yelled, getting off a shot before ducking back behind a corner.

Almost instantaneously, Hutchinson had squeezed the trigger. The sound he heard—the one that a minute earlier had been a life-saving reprieve—now made him sick: *Click!* The veteran cop had made a rookie mistake. He had forgotten to take the safety off the shotgun.

Before Hutchinson could do anything, Stewart's bullet struck the agent in the right arm, just below the shoulder, shattering it so badly that he thought it had been blown off. He didn't realize that the impact had caused his arm to end up draped over his shoulder blade.

The pain was the worst he had ever felt in his life. Dropping the shotgun, Hutchinson staggered back onto the landing and out to the carport.

There, he found Francom still lying on the ground where he had been left. With glazed eyes, Francom looked up and mumbled, "Sarge, I can't feel my legs."

Thank goodness, he's still conscious, Hutchinson thought. Despite the four bullet wounds, including two on his left side, Hutchinson used his left hand to drag his severely injured fellow agent down the driveway to the street.

To his shock, Hutchinson felt bullets whistling past him again. He turned around and saw Stewart standing on the front porch, shooting at him and the other agents who had taken up positions outside.

Hutchinson tottered into the street, dropped down, tucked Francom by the curb next to a gutter, and laid down beside him, hoping it would provide some semblance of protection. By now, Hutchinson was in agony and feeling light-headed. When Stewart stopped firing from the porch and headed for the backyard, Hutchinson went over to Rounkles's cruiser, plopped down on the opposite side for cover, and leaned his back against it. He was having trouble breathing from the wound in his rib and was getting increasingly dizzy from the loss of blood.

One of his fellow agents, Matt Jensen, helped Hutchinson to his feet and laid him down in the backseat of Rounkles's car. He put the barely conscious Burrell on top of Hutchinson. Another agent, Derek Draper, then slid into the front seat and headed to McKay-Dee Hospital. Meanwhile, Jensen carried Francom for an entire block to a waiting ambulance, which couldn't get any closer to the crime scene due to the ongoing gunfight.

Because members of the unit didn't drive patrol cars, Draper was unfamiliar with Rounkles's vehicle. As he sped down the side streets, he complained, "I'm driving as fast as I can, but I can't find where to turn on the siren and lights."

"No problem, Derek," Hutchinson said. "We're fine. Not to worry."

With Burrell on top of him, Hutchinson saw that his buddy's eyes were open and looking at him. "Hey, Kasey, we're going to make it," Hutchinson said. "We're going to be okay."

But Burrell wasn't talking or responding in any way.

Just when Hutchinson thought the pain from the bloody wounds in both hips and both arms couldn't get any worse, it did. But he forced himself to remain calm. He recalled what an instructor had said at a training session about getting shot: "Surviving a shooting has a lot to do with your mind-set. You can will yourself to live or will yourself to die. Your body can take a lot more trauma than you think. The bullet that you feel likely won't kill you; it's the bullet that you don't feel that will." *Well, I must be okay because I sure feel the pain from those bullets,* thought Hutchinson.

He also knew from training that if you can get to the hospital, your chances of survival are pretty good. *I think we're all going to make it. Shawn was walking and Jared was talking when I last saw them. Kasey has his eyes open, so that's a good sign.*

When the car arrived at the hospital, Draper ran inside, returned with a wheelchair, put Burrell in it, and hustled him into the emergency room. Hutchinson sat up in the backseat and noticed that his right arm had flopped down. *Well, that's good news. My arm isn't blown off after all. It's still here.*

With some difficulty, he got out of the car and staggered into the ER. He wobbled past a security guard who was sitting by the front door. So shocked to see a man bleeding from four wounds, the guard didn't say a word or get up. He just stared at him.

Well, if you're not going to help me, I'm going to keep walking, Hutchinson thought. He trudged to the nurses' station and once again was met by silent stares from personnel too stunned to move. *I guess I'll have to keep walking until I find an open room with a bed and lie down.* He was exhausted and in excruciating pain. Just when he thought he couldn't take another step, a nurse ran up from behind, helped him into a wheelchair, and put him into a room where a trauma team soon tried to stabilize him.

While lying in bed, Hutchinson thought of his family—his wife, two boys, 12 and 10, and 6-year-old daughter. He managed to get his cell phone out of his pocket and called them because he wanted them to hear what happened from him rather than from the news or someone else. He told them his injuries were serious but nothing that couldn't be treated. He assumed all his comrades had survived the shooting.

The next morning, before Hutchinson was wheeled in for surgery, his commander, Lieutenant Darin Parke, came to his room and delivered devastating news: Jared Francom was dead. The 30-year-old agent had been shot seven times.

Hutchinson could hardly believe it; in fact, he didn't want to believe it. *No, not Jared. He's too tough to die.* He was a weight lifter and bodybuilder, an adrenaline junkie who loved sky-diving and motorcycles. The two had been exceptionally close friends on and off duty and had joined in family barbecues and family outings. *No, not Jared.* Hutchinson felt crushed, as though he had lost a beloved brother. In a way, he had.

Parke also told him that Burrell had been put into a medically induced coma, adding, "We don't know how well he'll recover until after he comes out of it. Shawn [Grogan] is doing okay, but he's looking at multiple surgeries to fix his face."

Until Parke filled him in, Hutchinson wasn't aware that Rounkles and Vanderwarf had been shot. Although Rounkles's wounds were serious, he was expected to make a full recovery. Vanderwarf sustained only a superficial wound.

Parke reported that Stewart had holed up in a backyard metal shed, drawing concentrated gunfire from police. After suffering two bullet wounds, he had surrendered.

Grieving for his friend but also grateful that his other comrades would survive, Hutchinson underwent surgery to remove the bullets in his body and to repair his right arm. After spending a week in the hospital, he was told that he could go home.

A doctor then removed a port that had been inserted in the agent's neck right after he had been brought into the ER.

"What was that for?" Hutchinson asked. "You never used it for anything, so why did you put it in me?"

"The body isn't designed to take as much trauma as you suffered," the doctor replied. "We thought you likely would go into shock and cardiac arrest. We put the port in you so if your heart stopped, we could pump it full of steroids and try to get it started again. You were close to dying because it was looking pretty grim for a while."

Hutchinson shook his head. "I never thought I was going to die."

"Well, that's a big part of why we never needed to use the port. You never thought you would die, so you didn't."

Shortly after Hutchinson went home to begin a long and difficult recovery, he received a call from his boss, Sheriff Terry Thompson, who told him, "No one is going to think twice if you don't want to go back to the strike force. Everyone would understand."

Hutchinson replied, "Listen, Sheriff, it has never crossed my mind that I wouldn't return to the strike force. Not only do I want to go back, but I *need* to go back to the life I had before the shooting. I still love this job."

Hutchinson suffered a series of medical setbacks throughout 2012 caused by recurring infections in his wounds. He underwent eight surgeries, requiring plates, screws, and rods, to repair and rebuild his right arm. He has limited motion in that arm and can't raise it above his head. Because he lost most of his hearing from the loud din of the gunshots, he wears hearing aids and is considered legally deaf. The injury to his arm required him to make some adjustments on how to hold his gun, but he has passed the twice-yearly qualification shoot required of all police officers.

An estimated 4,000 people, including hundreds of officers from around Utah and other states, attended Jared Francom's funeral. American flags lined the seven-mile route of the procession, which involved 500 police vehicles. Francom was buried with full honors featuring a 21-gun salute, an aircraft flyover, and a final 10-42 call over the police radio, signifying an end of a shift. Francom, who left a wife and two young daughters, was the first police officer slain in the line of duty in Ogden in nearly 50 years. The name of the Ogden police headquarters was changed to the Francom Public Safety Building in 2013.

"It's hard," Hutchinson admits. "I still miss Jared. I think about him all the time. There isn't a day that goes by that I haven't thought of that night in one sense or another."

All other officers who survived the shooting that fateful night eventually returned to the strike force, but later moved on to other positions.

After spending another year on the strike force, Hutchinson was promoted to lieutenant and later made Commander of Professional Standards and Training. He still has the dented badge that deflected a bullet during the gunfight.

By 2015, all the others who were wounded were members of the Ogden Police Department. Kasey Burrell, who lay in a coma for two weeks, doesn't remember anything about the gun battle from the time he was shot until he woke up. Recovered from the gunshot wound to the head and other injuries, he's a master police officer in the Ogden Police Department's community policing program. Shawn Grogan, who sustained injuries to his face, is a master police officer in the patrol division. Michael Rounkles, who suffered several severe wounds, is a master police officer in the metro gang unit. Jason Vanderwarf, who recovered from his gunshot wound, is a detective.

Said Weber County attorney Dee Smith at the time, "To me, it's amazing they're all back to work and willing to continue to serve and protect this community after going through that. It says a lot to me of their character and their strength that they're still working with us."

Matthew David Stewart was charged with one count of aggravated murder, seven counts of attempted murder, and one count of producing a controlled substance. Prosecutors planned to seek the death penalty. Investigation revealed that he fired 31 shots from his 9-mm Berretta, 17 of which struck officers. Stewart claimed he fired at the police because he mistook them for home invaders trying to rob him. In May 2013, while awaiting trial, he hanged himself with a bedsheet in his cell at the Weber County Jail.

For running directly in the line of fire to rescue others in the fierce gunfight, Hutchinson was named Officer of the Month for March 2013 by the National Law Enforcement Officers Memorial

Fund. He also was awarded the Law Enforcement Congressional Badge of Bravery, which was presented to him by Utah Senators Orrin Hatch and Mike Lee. "Lieutenant Hutchinson is a man of honor and courage," Hatch said. Hutchinson received several other state and national awards, including the first-ever Medal of Honor given by the sheriff's office.

At a White House ceremony in 2015 honoring 22 law enforcement and firefighter heroes, Vice President Joe Biden presented Hutchinson with the Medal of Valor, the nation's highest award for public safety officers. "I was overwhelmed," Hutchinson recalls. "I never felt like I had done anything above and beyond or more special compared to anyone else. I was humbled by the award. I felt like I received it for all the officers who showed exceptional bravery that night—and Jared as well. Truly, everybody stepped up, not just me.

"I hope all the awards can show my children that good things can come from bad situations. I wish that night hadn't happened, but it did and I have to deal with it. I could dwell on the fact that my arm will never be the same and that I lost my hearing and that I was in and out of the hospital for a year, and I could stay angry forever at the guy [Stewart]. But I've chosen to move forward and be positive because I have a lot of life left to live."

BRIDGE OVER TROUBLED WATERS

OFFICER JESSE TURANO
Port Authority Police Department (New York)

His head down and his hands stuffed in his pockets, a middle-aged man scurried along a closed walkway on the George Washington Bridge, occasionally glancing at the dark, swirling waters 200 feet below. He refused to heed Port Authority Officer Jesse Turano's commands to stop.

Turano knew why the man was ignoring him. *He's going to try to kill himself,* thought the officer, tailing him. *Well, not on my watch.*

The man peered over his shoulder at the cop and then quickened his pace. Turano started trotting to shorten the distance between them, all the while yelling for him to stop. Turning around and seeing the officer closing in on him, the man paused, faced the river, and then started to vault over the railing—the last barrier between him and certain death.

Without worrying about his own safety, Turano rushed forward. His only thought: *Can I grab him in time?*

*   *   *

The George Washington Bridge, or the GW as it's often called, spans about three-quarters of a mile over the Hudson River, connecting upper Manhattan to Fort Lee, New Jersey. Every year, more than 100 million vehicles travel across its 14 lanes—8 on the upper level and 6 on the lower—making it the busiest bridge in the world.

With its twin 600-foot-tall towers of steel lattice on either side of the river, the dramatic double-decker suspension bridge has been a favorite backdrop in dozens of films. It has attracted millions of cyclists, walkers, joggers, and sightseers who crowd its south walkway.

Sadly, the bridge also has become a tantalizing draw for disturbed people who want to jump to their deaths. From 2010 through 2015, an average of 15 people committed suicide there each year.

It's a horrible way to die.

Leaping from the bridge into the treacherous river 20 stories below, a jumper of average weight will reach speeds of between 55 and 60 miles an hour. In slightly under three seconds, the person will crash into the water at about 30,000 pounds of force, causing catastrophic internal injuries that almost always lead to a painful death.

When Turano joined the Port Authority Police Department, he took to heart the law enforcement motto "To serve and protect." But during his five years patrolling the bridge from 2010 to 2015, he discovered that some of the people he would ultimately protect would be from themselves.

Twelve times, he risked his own life to physically thwart—at the last possible moment—a troubled individual from attempting a fatal plunge. And countless other times on the bridge, he prevented a suicide after spotting, and then talking with, a distressed person who was contemplating ending it all.

In 2006, the New Jersey–born former Marine joined the Port Authority of New York & New Jersey's 1,700-person police force, which oversees airports, bridges, tunnels, marine ports, railway systems, and commerce centers. During this time, the five-foot ten-inch, 220-pound officer competed in bodybuilding events, regularly working out with weights. His strength gave him an advantage over bad guys who needed to be physically restrained. That same strength helped save suicidal people from taking their lives.

In 2010, when he was 30 years old, Turano was assigned to a unit that patrolled the GW. It was the same year that a college student who had been cyberbullied jumped off the bridge in a suicide that attracted national coverage in the news and on social media.

The unwanted notoriety led some mixed-up copycats to view the George Washington Bridge as a good place to kill themselves. Alarmed by the increase in suicide attempts, the Port Authority stepped up the number of patrols by car and by foot on the GW.

But the hopeless and the despondent were still trying to leap off the bridge.

At about 10:00 p.m. on April 30, 2013, while patrolling the GW in his squad car, Turano received a call that a man had slipped past a civilian security guard on the east, or New York, side and entered the bridge's upper-level north walkway, which was closed to pedestrians. Turano thought, *He's trespassing and has no reason to be there—unless he's planning to jump.*

Searching the upper level in his squad car, Turano soon observed a middle-aged man with his head down and his hands in his pockets walking westward. The officer steered his cruiser into the lane closest to the walkway, slowed down, and when the car was even with the man, tried to get his attention by turning on the siren and flashing the roof lights. The man ignored him.

Driving alongside the man, Turano lowered the passenger window and shouted several times at him to stop. The man glanced at the cop and then turned his head away and kept on walking.

Something definitely isn't right, Turano thought. *He looks emotionally disturbed.* The officer parked his cruiser, hopped out, climbed over a low wall that separated the roadway from the walkway, and headed toward the man, whose back was to him. *He has his hands in his pockets, and I don't know what's in them. If he's suicidal and has a gun, he might pull it out and force me to shoot him.* The officer wanted nothing to do with a suicide by cop.

"Stop!" Turano ordered. "And get your hands out of your pockets!"

After a quick glimpse at the officer behind him, the man walked faster, so Turano broke into a run. Suddenly, the man stopped and gripped both hands on the railing on the waterside of the walkway. The railing topped a three-foot-high cement wall. He put his feet on top of the wall, pushed off, and began to hurdle over the railing.

In that one crucial second when the man was momentarily suspended above the railing, seemingly having leaped free of the bridge, Turano lunged for him. The officer's right arm grabbed him around the waist. The cop's left hand clutched the man's belt. For another second, the man, who weighed about 180 pounds, dangled over the side struggling to free himself. "No! No!" he shouted.

But the powerfully built Turano had a strong grasp of the man. *You're not going anywhere. I'm not going to let you go.* With a loud grunt, the officer leaned back and, using his body weight, pulled the man over the railing. Both fell onto the walkway. The man flailed away, but the officer quickly overpowered him and cuffed him for both their protection.

Turano then radioed for an ambulance. By the time EMS arrived, the man, a 40-year-old resident of nearby Queens, had calmed down considerably and now seemed ashamed of himself. Turano went with him in the ambulance, as police did on all such situations.

On the way to the Bergen Regional Medical Center in Paramus, New Jersey, for a psychological evaluation, the man said he had been out of work for three years and was tired of looking for a job. "I'd had enough," he told Turano. "But I guess I shouldn't have tried jumping off the bridge. That wasn't very smart of me. Thanks for pulling me back."

"The best way you can thank me is to get the help you need," Turano told him.

Later, Turano's supervisor looked into the Port Authority records of recent attempted suicides on the GW and said, "That's the sixth would-be jumper you've saved this year."

Another time, Turano responded to a call of an emotionally disturbed man who was running around in traffic on the bridge near the New York tower. It was clear by the person's actions that he wasn't going to jump, but he was creating a danger to himself and others. Turano and his partners managed to subdue the man and call for EMS.

As they were putting him in the ambulance, Turano received word of a man who was getting ready to leap from the south walkway near the New Jersey tower. Because of the traffic tie-up, the officer figured he could make faster time by sprinting than he could by using his cruiser. Turano dashed toward the New Jersey tower and soon noticed a middle-aged man in a business suit who had just taken off his shoes. *Why do people who are going to commit suicide feel it's necessary to take off their shoes before they jump?* the officer wondered.

By the time Turano reached the scene, he was winded from running. He cautiously approached the well-dressed man, who was leaning over the water while on the outside of the railing but holding on to it with his hands behind him.

Standing with his bare heels on a six-inch-wide lip, he was poised to jump.

At first, the man was unaware of the officer's presence. But when he saw Turano, the man let go. Once again, Turano, with not a second to lose, sprang forward and snatched the man by the neck and pulled him back over the railing.

The man put up a token struggle, then quit fighting and wept bitterly. Turano called for an ambulance and accompanied him to the hospital. "I'm an investment banker," the man told him. "I got into a big argument with my boss, and it got so bad that I just couldn't handle it anymore and I wanted to kill myself."

"Jumping off a bridge is never the answer," Turano said. "With the proper counseling, you can go on to a good life."

The following day, Turano was in the Port Authority police station when the man walked in with his wife and two small children. He had come straight from the hospital and was still wearing the admittance band on his wrist. He went over to Turano, threw his arms around him, and sobbed. After the man composed himself, he blurted, "Thank you so much for saving my life."

"You have a wife and two beautiful little kids," Turano said. "If you ever feel like committing suicide, think of them. Nothing could be worth dying over and leaving them without a husband and father."

Fortunately for Turano, most of the suicides he prevented didn't reach the stage where he had to put his life in danger to save others from themselves.

After patrolling the bridge for so long, he had developed a sixth sense for singling out people on the walkway who were contemplating jumping but hadn't actually climbed over the railing. Even when he was driving by at 50 miles an hour, he could glance at pedestrians and tell by their body language and mannerisms if there was a suicidal person among them.

Generally, people use the walkway to get from point A to point B. Sometimes they stop in the middle of the span and take a picture or gaze at the stunning view of New York City. But occasionally Turano would spot someone ambling with little purpose and shoulders slumped, oblivious to the throng. Or he would notice a person leaning over the railing and staring at the water for an unusually long time as if deep in thought.

Whenever Turano identified a potential suicide victim, the officer would stop his squad car and have a little chat. Surprisingly, more times than not, the person told him the truth—that he or she was indeed thinking about ending it all. He encouraged the person to seek help immediately. If the person agreed, which was almost always the case, he would arrange for a transport to the hospital for an evaluation.

Turano learned early on that the dagger of despair stabs people of all walks of life—the wealthy and poverty-stricken, the young and the elderly, male and female. It cuts across all nationalities, races, and religions.

One day, while driving back and forth on the bridge, Turano noticed an older, fashionable woman on the walkway gazing at the river. He didn't think much of it, but a half hour later, when he saw her still at the same spot, he decided to investigate. He parked his cruiser and approached her.

"Hey, how are you doing today?" he said in a chipper voice.

"Fine, Officer," she answered, not making good eye contact.

"What brings you here?"

"Oh, I am just out for a walk. It's a beautiful day."

"Yes it is, but I've driven by here twice and noticed that you haven't left this spot. Are you sure everything is all right?"

She nodded, but not convincingly.

"Where do you live?" the officer asked.

"Park Avenue."

"Does anyone know you're out here?"

"My husband might."

"Mind if I talk to him?"

She dialed the number on her cell phone and handed it to Turano who, after introducing himself, told the husband, "I've found your wife on the GW, and she's been here for some time. Is this normal?"

"Oh, my God," the man gasped. "She told me she was going to jump off the bridge. I was just getting ready to go out and look for her. This isn't the first time she's tried to commit suicide. Whatever you do, don't let her out of your sight."

Turano arranged for her to be taken to the hospital for a psychological examination. He later learned that the woman, who was quite wealthy, had had a face-lift two years earlier. Even though she was attractive, she was convinced that the plastic surgeon had made her look ugly. Unable to cope with the change in her appearance, she had attempted to take her life.

Whenever Turano conducted a field interview of a suspected suicidal person, he would pry into the reason why the person was on the bridge. Sometimes it turned out to be nothing more than someone soaking up the view or looking for artistic inspiration or simply being lost.

On a brisk, drizzly day, he stopped a young woman who had trespassed onto the closed north walkway. She apologized and said she didn't realize she wasn't supposed to be there. Under further questioning, she said she was from Brooklyn and was out for a long walk. To Turano, she sounded fine, was pleasant, and looked him in the eye. He was about to let her go, when he thought, *Her story doesn't make a whole lot of sense.*

"You said you came out here for a walk," he told her. "But it was raining all morning, and it's drizzling and chilly now. You're telling me you came all the way from Brooklyn in this kind of weather to go for a walk on the George Washington Bridge?"

"Yes, that's right."

"Why would you do that on a day like today?"

"Because I felt like a walk."

"Who knows you're here?"

"No one."

"Do you have a boyfriend?"

"Yes."

He convinced her to call the boyfriend on her cell phone so the officer could speak to him. "Hey, bud, I found your girlfriend here on the closed walkway of the George Washington Bridge," Turano told him. "Is it normal for her to take walks this far from Brooklyn on such a lousy day?"

"She threatened to jump off the bridge, but I didn't believe her," the boyfriend said. "That's why she's there. She's going to try to jump!"

Turano persuaded her to go to the hospital for evaluation and called for an ambulance. *And to think I almost let her walk away,* he thought, shaking his head.

During Turano's time patrolling the GW, the Port Authority often received phone calls warning that a troubled relative or friend had threatened to jump off the bridge and was now missing. If there was a good description, Turano and his partners would sprint along the walkway in a frantic search for the person. More than once, Turano had to tackle an anguished suicidal man who, after seeing police, tried to run away.

One time, Turano was given the description of a car driven by a teenager who had just told his parents he was going to kill himself on the GW. Turano canvassed the parking area along the Hudson Terrace on the New Jersey side, looking for the vehicle. He found it before the young man even got out of the driver's seat. When confronted by Turano, the teen put up a fight but was quickly subdued and involuntarily taken to the hospital for a mandatory 48-hour stay.

When accompanying suicidal people on the ambulance ride, Turano saw a variety of reactions. Some ranted and raved, others cried, and some stared blankly at nothing. Then there were those who threatened to return to the bridge and finish what they had started to do.

Tragically, he faced people who were trapped in such a dark, hopeless place in their minds that no amount of love and concern, no amount of counseling and medication could release them from their personal hell. Three times, Turano helplessly watched a suffering person plummet to instant death.

In one of those cases, Turano and his comrades confronted a man on a six-inch-wide ledge on the other side of the railing on the north walkway at about 2:00 a.m. The man warned them, "Stand back or I'll jump." For the next 90 minutes, the police tried talking him out of killing himself. They even brought his best friend on scene in an effort to persuade him to seek help. Just when it looked like they were making progress, the troubled man talked to someone on his cell phone. Then he calmly put it down and, without another word, leaped off the bridge.

Of all the tortured souls Turano encountered who were on the wrong side of the railing ready to jump, he was never able to persuade them to abandon their plans to self-destruct. No one he talked to in these desperate situations voluntarily came back over. He had to use force. If he was within reach of them, he snatched them. Every time.

Take his last save, for example.

On the evening of February 17, 2015, Turano and his partner, Officer Brendan Mulderrig, received a call about a suspicious person who had left his vehicle unattended on the lower-level roadway of the bridge near the New York side. Within minutes, the officers discovered an abandoned 2011 Toyota but couldn't find the driver.

From experience, Turano suspected that the person who left the car was suicidal and was probably somewhere on a narrow maintenance catwalk below the roadway. Hoping they weren't too late, the cops split up and began searching for the driver. Over the din of the traffic above, Turano heard a man yelling angrily. Following the voice, the officer found a middle-aged man standing precariously on an eight-inch-wide horizontal beam about two feet outside the catwalk railing. Clad in a jacket and pajama bottoms, the man was shouting into his cell phone and crying hysterically.

The only way I'm going to get him is if I actually go over the railing and reach out and snatch him, Turano thought. *At least he's not a big guy.* As the officer came closer, the man noticed him for the first time and screamed, "Get away! Get away! All I want to do is die!"

Turano stopped and in a calm voice told him, "Relax. Relax. All I want to do is talk to you." The officer knew not to make any quick moves because he didn't want to spook him. *If he moves an inch or two to the right or left, he's gone.*

The man kneeled on the beam and continued to yell into his cell phone, giving Turano a chance to take a few steps. As has always been his personal rule, Turano would never try to grab a potential suicide victim unless the officer was positive he could save him. Turano inched closer.

"Get away!" warned the man, later identified as a 37-year-old resident of East Rutherford, New Jersey. He began cursing at the officer and kept his eyes on him.

Turano froze. *I'm close enough. Now I just have to wait for the right moment.* Patiently, he waited until the man turned his head away and looked down at his cell phone. Turano rushed forward, hopped over the railing, and with his left hand holding onto the railing, wrapped his muscular right arm around the man's neck in a tight headlock.

"No! No!" the man howled in protest, trying to wriggle out of the cop's grasp and throw himself off the beam. Turano was strong enough to haul the squirming man toward the railing. During the struggle, the officer climbed back over the railing and locked his legs on its vertical bars so the man couldn't pull him over in a deadly dual fall. Still holding him in a headlock, Turano clutched the man by the back of his pajama pants. Fighting to free himself, the angry man was dangling in midair when his pants began ripping.

You're not getting away from me, thought Turano. *I'm not going to let you die while I'm out here.* But then the officer felt a shooting pain boring into his straining back muscles. *My back is giving out.* Knowing he couldn't hold on much longer, Turano shouted at his partner who had approached from the opposite side of the catwalk, "Help me! Help me!"

Mulderrig raced over and tried to grab the man's legs, but the man kept kicking him. Finally, Mulderrig secured the legs, and the two officers then yanked him back over the railing and safely onto the catwalk. After a brief tussle, the pair handcuffed him and then summoned an ambulance, which took him to Englewood Hospital and Medical Center for treatment.

Once again, Turano had pulled a suicidal person back from the brink of certain death just as he had done so many times before.

Turano no longer works on the bridge. In 2016, he was promoted to detective and assigned to the Criminal Investigation Bureau.

He says he's proud that he stopped people from committing suicide, adding, "It's always good to save a life."

Turano credits his weight training and quick reflexes for successfully restraining would-be jumpers. "I never spent a lot of time trying to talk people off the bridge," he says. "I didn't want to give them too much time to think about what they planned to do. Even if they were determined to kill themselves, they were scared. And I was counting on that to buy me time to get closer to them and wait for my opportunity to grab them. But I would grab them only when I knew I could reach them. Once they were in my grasp, I was sure they weren't going to fall. I could never go to sleep knowing that I had latched on to somebody and then lost him."

The George Washington Bridge is now heavily patrolled and monitored. In addition to having squad cars cruising back and forth on the bridge, the Port Authority has assigned officers to stroll the walkway looking for, and then helping, pedestrians with signs of depression and disorientation.

The bridge also has a series of emergency telephone lifelines placed by the railings, providing direct links to suicide prevention counselors. As part of a $47 million project, the Port Authority is installing nine-foot-high fencing along both sides of the bridge. Also, strategically placed security cameras are monitored 24/7 by personnel trained to look for suspicious behavior.

UP IN SMOKE

DEPUTIES SCOTT BLIGH AND
GARY KNEESHAW
San Diego County (California) Sheriff's Department

As strong winds and rough air turbulence slapped at their patrol helicopter, Deputies Scott Bligh and Gary Kneeshaw caught their first sight of the smoke and flames rolling up the side of El Cajon Mountain. They knew this would be no ordinary rescue attempt.

There was nothing ordinary about trying to find and save two rock climbers who were trapped on a rock face in the path of a raging wildfire.

But for the deputies to reach them and safely pluck them off the slope would demand more than relying on piloting and navigating skills and training. It would demand from each aviator a strong backbone and even stronger nerves for what they were about to do—fly half-blind into choking smoke, tussle with treacherous winds, locate the couple, perch the chopper on the edge of a fire-ravaged slope too small to land on, load up one climber, and take off with little clearance between the rock face and the rotor blades. And then do it again for the other climber—all before the fast-moving flames devoured the area.

Bligh and Kneeshaw were steadfast in their willingness to push themselves and their aircraft to the max because failure meant likely death for the climbers—and, possibly, for the deputies themselves.

In 2010, the San Diego County Sheriff's Department operated five law enforcement patrol helicopters that assisted police in searching for criminals and rescuing people in trouble. In addition, the department also owned two larger choppers for rescues and fighting forest fires in a joint operation with the state agency, Cal Fire. The air unit, known as ASTREA (short for Aerial Support to Regional Enforcement Agencies), flew out of Gillespie Field, a few miles northeast of San Diego, California.

Although Bligh and Kneeshaw didn't fly together often, the two longtime deputies had great respect for each other. Bligh, 43, a former Navy helicopter pilot, had been flying choppers for the department for 5 years after doing stints in patrol cars, motorcycles, and detention centers for 10 years. Kneeshaw, 42, also had 15 years under his belt with the department, working in detention centers, patrol, and the K9 unit. In 2009, Kneeshaw became a tactical flight officer (TFO) for ASTREA, responsible in the cockpit for navigating, interacting with the ground units via the radio, operating a computerized moving map, directing a powerful spotlight known as the Night Sun, and handling an infrared camera.

Their two-seat aircraft was often dispatched for missions such as rescuing hikers lost in the mountains, kids stranded in the canyons, elderly trapped in snow, and undocumented immigrants injured in the desert. There was, however, one big drawback to this chopper. Those being rescued usually had to be flown out one at a time because of space, weight, and balance issues. The TFO would have to give up his seat and stay behind until each person was transported to safety. This sometimes required multiple trips before the TFO could get picked up.

On the morning of August 21, Bligh and Kneeshaw took off in their helicopter—its call sign ASTREA-1—to assist fellow deputies in the nearby city of San Marcos, searching for a suspect who had fled into a wooded area after stabbing a woman. It was a hot day, so for better ventilation, the aviators had taken the doors off the helicopter, which wasn't air-conditioned. The high temperatures, hard seats, loud engine noise, and constant vibration of the rotor blades always made for an uncomfortable flight, but they were used to it.

The two airborne deputies soon spotted a man who matched the suspect's description hurrying along a surface street. While ASTREA-1 observed the man from above, Kneeshaw worked the radio and directed officers on the ground until they apprehended him.

When the pair returned to their base, Bligh joked, "Looks like we've done our good deed for the day."

At about 1:30 p.m., they were at their desks monitoring radio calls when they heard that a wildfire had broken out near the south base of El Cajon Mountain. Because of its distinct rock face on the south side, the 3,675-foot-tall mountain, about

30 miles northeast of San Diego, is popular with rock climbers, who call it El Capitan or El Cap. Sheriff's Department choppers ASTREA-10 and ASTREA-12, piloted by Deputies Dave Weldon and Gene Palos, took off and joined several other helicopters and Cal Fire fixed-wing tankers to assist firefighters by making water drops on the rapidly spreading blaze.

With all the activity in the air, Bligh and Kneeshaw stayed put but continued to monitor the radio. Soon two rock climbers, André Doria and Meg Rippy, both 27-year-old graduate students at Scripps Institution of Oceanography, called 911 on a cell phone, reporting they were about three-quarters up the mountain. They said they were above the fire and felt safe for the moment but wanted authorities to know the couple's location—just in case. A short while later, they called 911 again, this time declaring they were in immediate danger of getting overrun by the inferno.

Hearing that the climbers were in peril, Bligh and Kneeshaw took off. They knew their MD 530F helicopter could land in a smaller area and pull off a speedier rescue than the larger fire-rescue choppers could.

Meanwhile, dispatch told Weldon, in ASTREA-10, that eight people and a dog were stranded at a ranch on a grassy plateau on the southeast side of El Cajon Mountain. They feared there wasn't enough time for them to drive off the mountain before flames blocked their only exit—a narrow, winding dirt road. Weldon flew to the ranch, loaded up the maximum number for his aircraft (four), and brought them to El Monte County Park near the south base of the mountain.

During the short flight back to pick up the rest at the ranch, Weldon learned the two rock climbers were now threatened by the rapidly advancing fire. He and his partner, Captain Todd O'Carroll, looked for the couple but were unable to locate them. Because many cell phones automatically provide latitude and longitude coordinates to 911 calls, Weldon pressed dispatch to get him the climbers' exact locale. ASTREA-10 then went on to retrieve the last four persons and the dog and deliver them to the park.

Dispatch was finally able to pinpoint the location of Doria and Rippy and relayed the coordinates to the various aircraft swarming over the fire. While Bligh and Kneeshaw flew around the north side of the mountain to stay out of the way of the water-dropping planes, Weldon and O'Carroll headed for the climbers' location.

They sighted Doria and Rippy waving at them on a sloping, rocky ledge thick with dry vegetation, directly in the path of the spreading flames 100 yards below them. While ASTREA-10 hovered directly over the two climbers, Weldon radioed Bligh and Kneeshaw the coordinates of the location of Doria and Rippy.

At 500 feet altitude, ASTREA-1 sped clockwise around the mountain until it faced the east side of the fire. Strong, gusty winds were blowing hard out of the southwest, whipping up towering flames fueled by parched brush. Fire loves to roar uphill, especially when pushed by the wind—and this inferno was doing just that, straight toward the climbers who were enveloped in yellowish-brown smoke.

Bligh never liked flying through smoke, especially when he didn't have a visual reference to the ground. But time was precious; he couldn't wait for the winds to blow it away. Bligh told Kneeshaw, "We'll have to go into the smoke, and we don't know exactly what we'll face until we get to the location. Gary, are you cool with this?"

The rule in the cockpit was "Two to go, one to say no." Both the pilot and the TFO had to agree to a plan. If one felt it was too dangerous, they would back off and try to figure out another way.

Without hesitation, Kneeshaw responded, "I'm good with it, Scott."

"If we go higher, we're not going to see anything that's below the smoke," Bligh said. "If we follow the mountain slope up at a height where I can still see the rocks below, we should be able to find them."

Because the doors of the helicopter were off, smoke and ash began darting into the cockpit. As ASTREA-1 rose up alongside the steep, rocky slope, Bligh had a frightening thought: *If the rotors hit the rocks on the side of the mountain, it'll be over for all of us.*

Even though their moving map indicated they were close to the climbers' location, Bligh and Kneeshaw couldn't spot them. Weldon then radioed ASTREA-1, "Hey, I can see you guys. I'm directly above you."

They looked out the window in the roof of the cockpit and, through the smoke, caught a glimpse of Weldon's chopper hovering about 100 feet above them.

"I can see the rock climbers from my vantage point," Weldon said. "Can you come up here?"

"Go ahead and clear out of there, and we'll be right up," Bligh responded.

ASTREA-1 was being rocked by gusts and violent updrafts, making it difficult for Bligh to maintain a steady climb. Flying through hot, smelly smoke, he tried to point the nose of the aircraft toward the mountain so it was in front of him, but the wind was treating the helicopter like a weather vane, pushing the tail toward the rock face.

Having no choice, Bligh steered the helicopter into the wind, which meant the tail was closer to the mountain than the nose was. The chopper rose until the deputies saw Doria and Rippy, as well as the advancing flames that were shooting skyward from the bottom of a draw.

There wasn't a place on the slope big enough for the helicopter to land fully on both its 10-foot-long skids. "I'll have to do a toe-in," Bligh said. That meant he was going to land with only the front part of the skids touching the slope and the rest of the skids hanging over the side of the mountain while he maintained power to the chopper. Although it's a hairy maneuver, Bligh had trained many times for this kind of landing. "Gary, are you good with that?"

"Yes," said Kneeshaw, who trusted Bligh's piloting skills. "I think we have enough time to get them out." *But barely*, he thought. *At least there should be time for two trips. But three is pushing it.* Because of electrical equipment and survival gear behind the aviators' seats, there was no space for either climber to get into the back. As the TFO, Kneeshaw knew he would have to jump out, load Rippy into his seat, and remain behind until Bligh could return for Doria and then come back in a third trip for him—if there was time.

Battling the wind and poor visibility, Bligh turned the chopper toward the mountain and moved closer to the ledge. He couldn't rush this maneuver because he knew if he miscalculated, the rotor blades would strike the rock face, which would spell doom for all. Facing a clearance of just three feet for the blades, he landed the copter with only the first two feet of the skids touching the ledge. Almost all of the chopper was suspended over the side.

Kneeshaw hopped out and made his way over to Doria and Rippy, who were huddled against the rock face, holding on to their climbing gear. "Drop all your equipment!" Kneeshaw shouted above the din of the chopper and the roar of the wind and fire. They tossed down their carabiners (metal loops), clips, ropes, chalk bags, and backpacks.

Working quickly, Kneeshaw guided Rippy to the chopper where she plopped into his seat. To save time, he buckled her in with only the lap belt and not the shoulder harness. Then he retreated with Doria and gave Bligh a thumbs-up. Only 20 seconds had elapsed since ASTREA-1 had landed.

As Rippy blew Doria a kiss, Bligh backed the helicopter away from the ledge, then peeled off to the west. Ten seconds later, they flew out of the smoke. He descended as fast as he could and decided against landing at the parking lot of nearby El Monte County Park. Hoping to shave off a few precious seconds for the return trip, he found the nearest piece of flat ground that was a safe distance from the fire and landed on a dirt field on the valley floor about a half mile east of the park.

Speaking to Rippy for the first time on the 90-second flight, he told her, "Get out!" As soon as Rippy's feet touched the ground, Bligh was airborne again, the lap belt flapping in the wind against the side of the helicopter. Rippy then walked to retrieve her car.

On the ledge, Kneeshaw was hoping that Bligh would hurry because the flames were getting much closer. *I don't know if there's enough time for a third trip,* he told himself. *The fire is advancing pretty fast.*

The hot air was blowing as if it came from a giant, invisible hair dryer. So much ash was spinning around that the smoke turned darker, and it was getting harder to breathe. Kneeshaw realized how much heat was rising from the canyon below because the half of his body facing the fire was noticeably hotter than the other side. Looking down the slope, he estimated that the flames were jetting 75 to 100 feet high.

This isn't looking good, he thought. Glowing debris from burning trees began flying at him and Doria. Using a handheld radio that was plugged into his helmet, Kneeshaw radioed Weldon, "ASTREA-10, ASTREA-1 Ground. We could really use a water drop. The fire is coming at us way too fast. We need to get out of here."

"ASTREA-1 Ground, ASTREA-10," Weldon replied. "It's looking bad. You might try to seek cover in a rock outcropping off to your right. Or, if necessary, you could move into the black."

Kneeshaw didn't like what he had just heard. "Move into the black" meant that, as a last resort, he and Doria would have to sprint through a curtain of flames on the front line of the fire and try to reach an area that had already burned itself out.

We're in deep trouble. I don't think we can move into the black and survive. But if we stay on the slope, we'll turn into crisps.

"We need to get out of here right now," Kneeshaw told Doria. "Let's go up."

They tried to scramble over boulders the size of cars, but it was just too difficult. Acting on another option, they began working their way laterally across the slope through dense, neck-high brush and around large rocks.

Kneeshaw radioed Bligh, "We're on the move to the west." There was no response. *Scott probably has his hands full.* The radio in the chopper was located on the TFO's side. *Maybe Scott is too busy to reach it. I hope that even though he's not responding, he can still hear me and knows what we're doing.*

Kneeshaw and Doria reached a spot 60 yards away where there was less smoke but more vegetation. *Will our new position make it harder for Scott to find us?* Kneeshaw worried.

Even though he heard plenty of radio traffic from all the aircraft in the area, he wasn't getting any response from anyone. Kneeshaw had an unsettling feeling that he was talking, but nobody was listening. He was beginning to wonder if he and Doria were on their own. *I'm not going to die on this mountain*, he vowed to himself. He had a wife and two beautiful young daughters waiting for him at home. *I'll run until I can't run anymore.*

When Bligh took off from the dirt field after dropping off Rippy, he was concerned that he wouldn't locate his partner or Doria in time, so he pushed the helicopter to its limits, and a little beyond. He wanted to change the radio frequency, but he was right at the edge of the chopper's performance, and he was afraid that if he let go with one hand the turbulence would cause the aircraft to fail.

Staring at the rock face, Bligh realized that from this vantage point, he didn't recognize the location where he had left Kneeshaw and Doria. *Everything is covered in smoke. How am I going to find them? There's no way.* For a fleeting moment, he felt defeated. But then he purged that negative thought and told himself, *I've got to take a shot at locating them, or they're pretty much done.* He hated the feeling of not knowing whether they were still alive.

He kept searching, hoping he'd catch sight of Kneeshaw's bright blue helmet or Doria's red one. Flying into the smoke, he could barely make out the rocks on the side of the mountain. His irritated eyes were watering from the scorching heat, blowing ash, and glowing embers, adversely affecting his vision. His face turned into a waterfall of tears that he couldn't wipe because the air turbulence forced him to keep both hands on the controls to maintain flight.

None of the other aircraft had reported sighting Kneeshaw and Doria since smoke shrouded the pair. Worried that the fire would overrun them, Weldon in ASTREA-10 called for firefighting helicopters to begin making water drops on the flames immediately below Kneeshaw's last known location. Deputy Gene Palos in ASTREA-12 moved into position to make the first drop.

Just then, Bligh caught a glimpse of red and blue. *Is it them?* His stinging eyes studied a bushy spot on the rock face, which was a different location than where he had left them. *Yes, it's them! That's the luckiest thing ever! What a relief. But it looks like the flames are closing in on them.*

"ASTREA-1, this is ASTREA-12," radioed Palos. "I'm ready to make my water drop."

"ASTREA-12, this is ASTREA-1," Bligh replied. "Go ahead and drop."

"I can't," said Palos. "You're in the way."

Fearing the smoke would again obscure Kneeshaw and Doria, Bligh responded, "I can't move away now. I'll never find them again."

"ASTREA-1, this is ASTREA-12. I'm aborting the drop. Go ahead and get them."

On the brushy slope, Kneeshaw kept his eyes peeled, waiting desperately for the chopper to emerge from the clouds of smoke. Suddenly, he saw a yellowish light appear through the smoke and become brighter. *It's the copter's landing lights. He's found us!* The helicopter broke through the brown smoke. *Oh, man, is it good to see him.*

"I see you!" Kneeshaw radioed Bligh. "We're off to your right!"

Even though there was no response, Kneeshaw was sure Bligh had heard him, or at least saw them, because the chopper turned and was now facing them. "I'm low on your nose!" Kneeshaw shouted in his mouthpiece. "I'm low on your nose!"

Kneeshaw motioned for Doria to follow him. The two moved another 10 yards to a better location where the vegetation wasn't so tall. *Okay, this is good. Scott is lining up for a toe-in.* Kneeshaw made Doria kneel down so there was no chance he would be struck by the rotor blades when Bligh touched down.

The chopper was 50 feet away, then 40, then 30. As it headed straight toward them, everything was looking good. And suddenly it wasn't. A powerful gust caught the tail and swung it dangerously close to Kneeshaw. In all his years around aircraft, he had never seen a helicopter make a 180-degree turn so swiftly. One moment, he was looking at the nose of the aircraft, and the next second he was facing the deadly rotors on its tail. He instinctively ducked. Then in an instant, the copter moved away from the mountain.

His heart sank. *Oh, my God, Scott can't make it. The wind is just too strong.* Kneeshaw immediately started looking around for an escape route. The smoke was billowing up, denser than ever. His eyes were stinging and tearing up as chunks of flaming pieces of branches swirled around him. *There's no way Scott will be able to get back to us. I don't want to try outrunning this fire, but I guess we'll have to.*

When the wind spun the chopper 180 degrees, a warning horn blared in the cockpit and the control panel lit up with three emergency alerts—low rotor RPM, engine out, and the engine reignition advisory. It was every pilot's nightmare. The instruments were alerting Bligh that the helicopter might not be airworthy. Refusing to panic, he let his training take over and quickly determined that he still had a working engine.

He backed the helicopter off about 50 feet from the mountain and stabilized the aircraft with some heavy-duty "pedal dancing"—busily operating the anti-torque pedals to regain control in the turbulent, smoky air. Once that crisis was over, he told himself, *Ignore all the warnings and try another toe-in. I have to get them out of there.* He estimated the flames were only 10 to 20 feet away from them.

Sweat and tears caused by the hot smoke were streaming down his face. Hot embers were blowing into the cockpit, pricking his cheeks even though his visor was down. Squinting, he could make out the colors of Kneeshaw's and Doria's clothes and bright helmets to help guide him through the smoke to their new location.

Flying half-blind, he moved in again for his second attempt at a toe-in. *I don't know if I have the clearance to do it. Go slowly, and hopefully my skids will hit the slope before the rotor blades hit the rock face. Otherwise, we're all done.*

Through the smoke, Kneeshaw saw the chopper's landing lights about 30 feet away. "It's Scott!" Kneeshaw shouted to Doria. "He's trying to make another toe-in!"

This time Bligh successfully placed the front 12 inches of the skids on the slope. Standing on the right skid, Kneeshaw helped Doria into the lone available seat. Doria scooted over toward Bligh, trying to make room for Kneeshaw. But Kneeshaw was afraid Doria would interfere with the flight controls that were situated between his seat and the pilot's. Kneeshaw pulled Doria back toward the center of the seat and strapped him in.

Looking over his shoulder, Kneeshaw realized that the flames were racing toward him. *There's not enough time for Scott to drop off Doria and return for me. I have to go with them now.* He would have to do something he had never done before during a rescue—fly on a helicopter while standing on the outside.

With his right foot on a step by the seat and his left foot on the skid, Kneeshaw leaned in and clutched the hand strap on the inside of the cockpit with his right hand. His left hand gripped an outside rack that held the Night Sun spotlight and infrared camera. "Go! Go!" he yelled to Bligh. "There's not going to be a third trip!"

Understanding how dangerous it was for Kneeshaw to be standing on a skid untethered, Doria put his arm through Kneeshaw's gun belt to hold him in place.

As soon as the chopper backed off the mountain, Kneeshaw noticed that the caution lights on the control panel were lit up. *Oh, great. Now the aircraft has mechanical problems.*

Ignoring the caution lights, Bligh thought, *All I have to do is back away and not hit anything, and we're good.* Despite the wind and turbulence, he deftly guided the aircraft off the mountain. Normally he would have ascended to get out of the smoke, but he figured it was too risky for Kneeshaw. *If I go up and Gary falls, he'll die. Better to stay low and follow the slope, so if he falls, at least he has a good chance of surviving.* Bligh remained within 15 feet of the sloping, rocky terrain and traveled much slower than he did for Rippy's flight. As much as all three wanted to get away from the fire and onto the ground as quickly as possible, Bligh told himself, *Take it slow and easy for Gary's sake.*

Spread-eagled awkwardly on the outside of the helicopter, Kneeshaw held on for dear life as the wind continued to buffet the aircraft. Most of his weight was being supported on his left leg, which began to quiver from the strain. He tried not to think about the reliability of the hand strap, which was nothing more than a piece of cordage held by two screws. It wasn't designed to hold someone who was hanging on while standing on a skid.

Kneeshaw peered under his arm. The rotor wash was whipping burning debris everywhere. Below, through the smoke, he saw towering flames twisting into the shape of orange tornadoes.

The bumpy ride took a couple of minutes—a long couple of minutes. When the helicopter finally landed near the park, Kneeshaw leaped off. It never felt better to be standing on firm ground.

"Congratulations on living!" Bligh shouted to Doria, who grinned at the remark.

After Doria was unbuckled, he got out and shook Kneeshaw's hand. Kneeshaw then escorted him to Rippy's car.

When Kneeshaw returned to the aircraft, he settled into his seat and buckled up. Neither he nor Bligh said anything at first. Without a word, Bligh stuck his hand straight out and showed his partner it was trembling. Then Bligh lifted his foot off the pedal. It was also shaky.

Kneeshaw cracked a knowing smile. He held out his hand to reveal it was unsteady, too.

After another minute of silence, Bligh said, "Are you ready to go?"

"Yeah," Kneeshaw replied. "I'm good with that. Let's go home."

*   *   *

Five days after the daring rescue, Bligh and Kneeshaw were honored with a commendation from the County Board of Supervisors at a press conference at Gillespie Field. Lieutenant Todd Richardson praised the deputies for actions "above and beyond the call of duty which, without a doubt, saved the lives" of the rock climbers, who attended the ceremony.

Rippy said she and Doria stayed calm while waiting to be rescued. "The biggest moment of fear was realizing we were surrounded by fire, and they couldn't see us in the smoke," she told reporters at the event. "We realize how very lucky we are to be here today." Turning to face the deputies, she added, "You are our heroes and saved our lives—and we thank you so much."

Doria, who estimated the couple lost more than $2,000 worth of equipment, praised the deputies for "their precise skills and amazing bravery."

In gratitude, he and Rippy later treated Bligh, Kneeshaw, and sheriff's fire rescue pilot Dave Weldon to dinner. The couple also sent thank-you notes and a photo of themselves to the aviators.

Kneeshaw, who keeps their picture in his office, recalls, "I went with my gut and believed that things would work out. I relied on my training, but I admit, I was scared. I don't want to ever have to repeat that rescue. I'm glad Scott was piloting that day, because he did a tremendous job."

"Every time I think about it, I feel my pulse race," Bligh admits. Recalling the harrowing moments when he was struggling for control of the helicopter while trying to pick up Doria and Kneeshaw, he says, "I was squeezing the controls so hard that if they had been living things, they would have been bleeding."

Bligh adds that when he returned home, he found his wife and two children splashing in the family pool. "I was still amped up by the rescue, so I jumped into the water with all my clothes on. I was just so glad I didn't turn my kids into fatherless children and my wife into a widow."

In his official report, Weldon wrote, "Both deputies showed incredible courage and valor in the face of what could have had disastrous results. In my opinion, the two hikers would not have survived the advancing fire had it not been for the impressive efforts of Deputies Bligh and Kneeshaw."

At a ceremony in Sacramento in 2011, Bligh and Kneeshaw were among 13 heroes who were awarded the Medal of Valor, California's highest honor for public safety officers.

Bligh was promoted to sergeant and put in charge of supervising the deputies in patrol cars while still attached to ASTREA. Kneeshaw, who was promoted to corporal, became qualified to fly helicopters and was named chief pilot of the unit.

The raging wildfire, which was started by two kids playing with matches, eventually burned 926 acres. Remarkably, no one was injured, especially the two rock climbers who owe their lives to a pair of brave deputies.

IN MORTAL DANGER

CORPORAL JUSTIN GARNER
Carthage (North Carolina) Police Department

Officer Justin Garner parked his police cruiser in front of Carthage Auto Glass and watched the Sunday traffic as the locals were going to and from church and the nearby McDonald's and Hardee's.

At this time of day, the 25-year-old officer was the only cop on duty in the 18-person police force because, well, there was little need for anyone else. Having been born and raised in Carthage, his hometown of 2,070 souls, Garner knew trouble seldom happened on Sunday mornings—or any other day, for that matter. Certainly the crimes in this Mayberry-like setting were nothing like the ones committed in big cities such as Charlotte, North Carolina, 90 miles west of here.

No, this was a quiet place, a throwback to a simpler time of an uneventful but rewarding life where everyone knew everyone and looked out for one another. Certainly on a national level, nothing newsworthy came out of Carthage.

But all that was about to change.

Within the next few minutes, this lazy Sunday morning of March 29, 2009, would turn horribly tragic by a senseless shooting spree that would leave many dead and traumatize not only the victims' loved ones but every resident in town. As shocking as it would become, the mass murder would have been much worse if not for the courage of the lone lawman.

At 10:01 a.m., the Moore County 911 dispatcher radioed Garner that someone had reported shots fired at 801 Pinehurst Avenue—the address of Pinelake Health and Rehabilitation Center, a sprawling facility that provided nursing care to seniors. The police had responded to calls like this every so often around the outskirts of town. *Maybe a target shooter in one of the nearby houses didn't realize that a few of his bullets were striking the building,* Garner thought. *Maybe a hunter in the woods got too close.*

Guns and the outdoors had always been a part of Garner's life. He grew up with a love for hunting and fishing. His father, Randy, a roofer, instructed him how to hunt deer with a bow and arrow and how to shoot with a rifle in the farmlands and forests outside Carthage. The boy was comfortable around guns and proved to be an excellent shot. He was an even better son. His mother, Debra, who taught at a small school started by their church, Rainbow Baptist, and his dad raised him right, because the clean-cut youth never got into a lick of trouble. No one in town had a bad word to say about Justin Garner.

Ever since he was old enough to dream about it, Justin wanted to become a police officer. He joined the town's volunteer fire department at age 17. Many of Carthage's firefighters also served as policemen, so the more he got to know them, the more he wanted to be a cop. Garner began his Basic Law Enforcement

Training (BLET) at Sandhills Community College when he was 19 so that he could land a job in the Carthage Police Department as soon as he turned 20. In 2005, a year after he had joined the force, he married his sweetheart from Union Pines High School. His bride, Stephanie, went on to study nursing.

Over the next few years, Garner lived the life of a small-town police officer, handling wrecks, fender benders, domestic issues, and drunks. He took the time to talk to people in the community and became adept at settling issues before they flared into arrests. The young cop so impressed his superiors that he was named Officer of the Year in his second year on the force.

Working various shifts and undergoing continuous training, Garner had one career ambition—to become a state trooper. He applied to the North Carolina State Highway Patrol but was turned down. Although disappointed, he remained dedicated to his job as a Carthage police officer in the town he loved.

After getting word from dispatch about shots fired at the nursing facility, Garner headed in his Dodge Charger cruiser for the mile-and-a-half run, but didn't put on his lights or siren. Even when dispatch called again and said there were multiple shots, he still assumed it was an innocent but careless mistake by a hunter or target shooter.

When he pulled up to Pinelake, he spotted a parked red Ford Ranger pickup. The driver-side window and back window had been shot out. *There's more going on than just a hunter*, he thought.

Getting out of his vehicle at the front entrance, he didn't hear any shots. As he reached the front door, a woman burst out, screaming, "There's a man inside, and he's shooting people!" She waved her arms in panic and ran off before he had a chance to stop and question her.

This clearly was no problem with a wayward hunter. This was an active shooter situation. Garner had undergone some training for this challenging scenario at a local middle school with five other officers. Instead of bullets, they used firecrackers to simulate gunshots and bombs. At the time, in BLET, the thinking was that with an active shooter, the first officer to respond should wait for backup and not go into a building alone. Because Garner never thought he would be put in such a dangerous position, he hadn't talked about this kind of situation with his comrades.

On his shoulder mic, he asked dispatch if any backup was on the way. He didn't hear any response. Waiting for backup crossed his mind for just a second. As the only officer on duty in town, he told himself, *There's no way I'm going to wait. I have to go in right now.*

He pulled out his Glock 40. It had a bullet in the chamber and 14 more in the magazine. He cautiously entered the rehab center and instinctively touched his body armor for a little reassurance.

Inside, he was met with silence, dead silence. There were offices to his left and right, a hall table ahead of him, another room off to the right, and a dining hall farther down. No one was at the front desk. *There's definitely something bad going on here.*

The first person Garner saw was an elderly woman slumped over in her wheelchair, which was in a pool of blood. When he checked on her, he discovered she had been shot in the thigh and had bled out. *She's gone. Why would anyone shoot a little old lady in a wheelchair? I have to find this guy.*

Garner took pride in remaining calm, even in stressful situations. Not an excitable person, he took a couple of deep breaths and reminded himself that if he ever needed to be composed, this was the time. But it was still hard to believe that a murderer was on the loose here in little Carthage, North Carolina. *Can this really be happening?*

What scared him the most was not knowing where the shooter was or what the guy was doing or planned to do. Then another frightening thought came to him: *Could there be more than one shooter?*

He moved deeper into the center, aware that the gunman could be lurking anywhere. Holding his gun in a two-handed, ready-to-shoot grip, Garner began doing a slow walk, carefully opening each door to see if anybody was inside. *Take your time,* Garner told himself. *I can't pass a door and not check it, because I don't know if he's in one of them, ready to shoot me in the back.* Some rooms were empty. In others, an unaware patient was lying in bed. In one of the hallways, he saw elderly people wandering around, clueless to the danger they were in. *They're like children—totally defenseless.*

No one said a word to Garner as he continued to peek into each room. However, one alert patient in a wheelchair at the end of a hallway pointed toward the kitchen area.

Garner walked toward a nurses' station where several hallways branched off. His head swiveling, he kept looking and listening for any sign of the killer. He had yet to hear any gunfire. As he moved down the hallway, he could feel the tension mount. *Where is he? I have to stop him before he kills again. Where is he?*

When Garner reached the nurses' station, his eye caught movement on the other side in another hallway. A wide-eyed middle-aged man was standing in front of a room, his arms up, gesturing to the officer that he wasn't the shooter. He was just a visitor—a terribly frightened one. He pointed down the hall and mouthed the words, "He has a gun."

Garner was still clearing rooms when suddenly he was jolted by a series of deafening gunshots—*Boom! Boom! Boom! Boom!*—coming from another hallway. Garner knew weapons. *That's the sound of a shotgun,* he thought. It was so loud it sounded to the officer as if someone had stuck the barrel of a shotgun down a 50-gallon drum and fired. *I have to find where the shots are coming from.*

Garner quickened his pace. He turned down a hallway, which flowed into another hall that led to the locked Alzheimer's ward. And then he saw him.

Standing outside the ward with his back turned to Garner, a man with a shotgun was trying to get into the ward but couldn't, even after blasting away at the door. When the man was unable to enter, he rested the shotgun on his left shoulder, turned around, and entered the long hallway that Garner was in.

From the far end, the officer caught his first good look at the gunman—a large, bearded man wielding a Mossberg 12-gauge shotgun. A bulging ammo bag was slung over his shoulder.

"Drop your gun!" Garner ordered, pointing his Glock at the man.

Without uttering a word, the assailant stared at the officer and began calmly reloading his weapon with cartridges filled with buckshot—big metal balls designed to bring down deer. The shotgun was pointed at the ceiling while he chambered a shell into the weapon.

"Drop your gun!" Garner commanded again.

Ignoring the order, the man kept staring at him until the gun was reloaded. Then he began walking toward the cop.

"Drop your gun!" Garner shouted for the third time.

The man not only refused to comply with the order but was now lowering his weapon into a shooting position by his shoulder and aiming it directly at Garner, 100 feet away.

The young officer had never fired his Glock at another person; he had never even shot it while on duty other than at a firing range. *Am I going to have to shoot him? I definitely want to go home to my wife, but if I don't take action right now, I might not come home.*

He was now staring directly at the gun of the killer. *Bang!*

*　　*　　*

Robert Kenneth Stewart, 45, of Carthage, was a burly, emotionally troubled house painter who was chronically short on money but always seemed to have enough for booze. He had been married and divorced several times and wanted to get back with his ex-wife Wanda, 43, who worked as a certified nursing assistant at Pinelake.

After she spurned him because of his violent behavior and excessive drinking, he became enraged and, in his twisted mind, planned to murder her. Knowing she would be working in the Alzheimer's unit at Pinelake that fateful Sunday, he drove to the nursing facility, which had no security guards. He brought with him a .22-caliber rifle, a shotgun, an ammo bag crammed with more than five dozen shells, and a revolver in a holster on his back.

When Stewart arrived at the parking lot shortly before 10:00 a.m., he went over to Wanda's unoccupied car and blew holes in its doors and shattered its windows with his rifle. Unaware of the shooting, Michael Cotten, 53, drove up in a red pickup truck to visit his ailing great-aunt. The deranged Stewart shot at the truck three times, demolishing the driver-side window and back window and wounding the man in the shoulder. Cotten leaped out of his pickup. But instead of running away, he boldly sprinted past Stewart and into the nursing home to warn the staff about the gunman.

Registered nurse Jerry Avant, Jr., 39, immediately sounded the alarm over the intercom that a shooter was entering the building and told coworkers to move patients into rooms and lock all doors. In the Alzheimer's unit, which was protected by a passcode and a timed lock, staffers herded patients into a TV room, where they barricaded the door, pulled the blinds, and ordered everyone to remain quiet. Wanda hid in a bathroom. In other wings of the facility, staffers hurriedly guided patients into rooms and out of the hallways. But there were several elderly people that staffers couldn't reach in time to help.

Once inside the facility, Stewart calmly and deliberately began blasting away with his shotgun, killing people at point-blank range. The first victim—the one Garner discovered was dead—was Louise De Kler, 98, who had been waiting in the entrance hall for her daughter to take her to Sunday lunch. Lillian Dunn, 89, who had been sleeping in her wheelchair near a nurses' station, was the next one murdered.

As Stewart calmly strolled down the hall, he indiscriminately fired at some people and spared others. He opened doors to rooms and shot patients while they lay in their beds. When Avant confronted him, Stewart shot him in the leg and again in the chest.

Staffers who had barricaded themselves in closets and behind locked doors began calling 911, pleading for help. The first call came in at 10:01, but the message that dispatch gave Garner didn't indicate the shooter was inside the building.

Then came other calls, including this from a petrified woman: "There's a man in here with a double-barreled shotgun shooting people . . . a white man with a beard . . . Please hurry up!"

Even the wounded Avant contacted 911, saying, "Y'all need to get over here to Pinelake."

"We've got help on the way, sir," the operator replied.

"I've been shot. I've already been shot."

Visitor Michael Gillis, who had brought his wife, mother, stepfather, and sons, ages 17 and 9, with him to see his bedridden grandmother, hadn't reached her room yet when Cotten dashed past them, shouting, "There's someone with a gun!"

Hearing the gunshots, Gillis shepherded his family into his grandmother's room and shut the door before rushing them into her bathroom. It had no lock, but the door was metal. He told his eldest son, "Hold the handle so no one can get in. If someone shoots the door, it's going to hurt, but you'll be okay. You hold that handle until you hear the sound of my voice."

Then Gillis closed the bathroom door and stood beside his grandmother, ready to defend her even though he was unarmed. He heard the gunshots and the squeaking of Stewart's shoes as the crazed killer strolled down the hall. When Gillis assumed that Stewart had gone past the room, Gillis opened the door and stepped out, planning to tackle the gunman. But then Stewart turned and reloaded his shotgun. Gillis ducked back into his grandmother's room, slammed the door, braced himself, and thought, *Oh, this is going to hurt.*

But Stewart didn't shoot through the door. Instead, he walked down the hallway.

Telling his grandmother to stay put and not call his name, Gillis went out and saw Stewart shoot into a patient's room on one side, then turn and shoot a woman in her doorway on the other side. Gillis watched Stewart point the weapon at another woman but not shoot. There seemed no rhyme or reason as to who lived and who died. Stewart walked by just as many as he shot.

Gillis planned to follow Stewart but then saw Garner coming toward him, pistol drawn. Fearing the officer might mistake him for the shooter, Gillis threw up his hands, pointing one finger to the left where Stewart was disappearing around the corner at the end of the hallway. To the cop, Gillis mouthed, "He has a gun."

As he stared at the barrel of Stewart's shotgun, Garner was frozen in place in a shooting position. His legs were spread and both hands were gripping his Glock. He was aiming for a center mass shot, Stewart's chest area. Garner squeezed the trigger.

Stewart fired, too. Garner never heard the blast of the shotgun because the noise was masked by his own gunfire. Both men had shot at the exact same moment.

Garner winced when he felt pellets striking his left leg and left foot. *I need to get behind some cover.* He stepped to his left and into an empty patient's room, which had a partially opened door. *At least I have something to protect me.* After a few seconds of silence, he wondered, *Did I hit the guy?* Garner was a crack shot and was fairly certain that he indeed had shot the killer. *But what if I missed? Then he's coming after me. I have to find out.*

The officer peered out from behind the door and saw Stewart sprawled belly-down on the floor with arms out-stretched in front of him. The shotgun was lying three feet away from him. *Yep, I shot him.* Garner's lone bullet had hit Stewart right where the young cop had aimed—below the gun-man's armpit and above the breastplate by the heart.

Ignoring his own bleeding wound, Garner ran toward Stewart, who was groaning. After kicking the shotgun farther away from Stewart, Garner ordered, "Put your hands behind your back!" Like before, Stewart didn't comply. Garner repeated the command. This time, Stewart slowly did what he was told, and Garner cuffed him.

From the time Garner had received the first call about gunshots until he subdued the killer, only five minutes had elapsed.

He radioed dispatch from his shoulder mic and reported, "Shots fired. Subject down."

"Copy that," replied dispatch, known as Central. "Have you located the shooter?"

"Ten-four," replied Garner, using the police code for yes. "He's down, Central. He's been shot, and I've been shot in the foot."

"All units, be advised officer has been shot."

Once Stewart was cuffed, Garner noticed the killer had a .38-revolver in a holster tucked in his lower back. Garner pulled the weapon out of the holster, took out the bullets and put them in his pocket, and placed the gun on a nurse's tray. Then he unloaded the shotgun, pocketed those shells, and leaned the weapon against the wall in the hallway.

"Are you by yourself?" Garner asked.

"Yeah," Stewart replied before muttering, "Kill me. Just kill me."

Garner slipped Stewart's wallet out of his back pocket and looked at his ID. The officer didn't realize it at the time, but he had seen Stewart eight years earlier when they were members of the same hunting club.

As he waited for backup to arrive, Garner shook his wounded leg and saw buckshot fall out and bounce on the floor. Only three pellets penetrated his leg—one in his calf muscle, one in the front, and one that struck his shin and became lodged behind the bone. Another pellet hit his boot and went into his heel. He felt some pain, but it was tolerable, mainly because of the adrenaline flowing through him.

Garner remained in the hallway until a sheriff's deputy and a cop from nearby Whispering Pines arrived. At Garner's request, they went room to room to see who was alive and who was dead.

By 10:06 a.m., ambulances were rushing to the scene, followed quickly by additional police. Four minutes later, Garner reported that the scene was secure and the building was safe for other deputies to enter.

After the shooting, staffers and visitors who had hunkered down came out to check on the patients. The building reverberated with hollering, screaming, and crying. A nurse ran by Garner. She was sobbing and shrieking as she rushed to the side of her fiancé, Avant, who was lying on the floor at the end of a service hall after getting shot multiple times.

Gillis was already kneeling by Avant, who had been caring for Gillis's grandmother for weeks. "Jerry, what can I do?" Gillis asked.

"Nothing," Avant gasped. "I'm going to die."

After going to the hospital for treatment of his wounds, Garner returned to the scene of the mayhem where Carthage Police Chief Chris McKenzie had set up a command post. It was only then that the chief told Garner the full scope of the murderous rampage: Stewart had killed eight innocent people—seven residents, ranging in age from 78 to 98, and Avant—and had wounded three others, including Garner. Stewart's wound wasn't life-threatening and he was expected to make a full recovery.

"Eight people dead?" Garner said in stunned surprise. "It's hard to believe that many were killed."

"Justin," the chief said, "there would have been many more helpless people murdered if you hadn't acted the way you did. He had plenty of ammunition and was going to do massive damage. No one else was killed after you went in here alone. If that's not heroic, I don't know what is."

Not until Garner returned home later that night did the tragic events of the day sink in. "I had a hard time dealing with the fact that this guy tried to kill me," Garner recalls. "Every time I closed my eyes, I saw him reloading that gun and staring at me. That lasted quite a while.

"It was scary. Very scary. I never expected something like that. But really, I didn't have a whole lot of time to think about it. I just had time to react."

In the week following the massacre, Garner received more than a thousand messages from people expressing gratitude and support. Letters poured into the police station from as far away as England, praising the young cop. "At a memorial service later, staff members and families of the patients came up and thanked me," Garner says.

In September 2009, Garner, who was promoted to sergeant, was awarded the National Tactical Officers Association Individual Medal of Valor. He also received numerous other honors and was commended on the floor of the US House of Representatives.

Chief McKenzie told the press, "I don't know that anybody can understand what it takes for a single officer to enter a facility alone with a gunman on the loose and to forge ahead and do his job. No matter how much training an officer has, it's hard to shoot accurately in a moment of mortal danger. It takes a lot of control and steadiness to hit a man at 35 yards with a single pistol shot—especially when the bad guy is shooting back."

After Garner's heroic actions, Basic Law Enforcement Training changed its advice. If a police officer arrives at an active shooting situation alone, he or she should not wait for backup. Instead, the officer should go in alone because, in this case, seconds count and confronting the shooter can mean the difference between life and death. As one instructor put it, "You have to engage the killer as quickly as possible. If the killer is killing, kill the killer."

Garner did a training video about this scenario. All students enrolled in BLET in North Carolina are required to watch the video as part of the course.

The next time that Garner saw Stewart was at his murder trial in 2011 when the officer testified against the defendant. Stewart was at a table with his head down and wouldn't look at him. The defense contended that Stewart wasn't responsible for his actions the day of the killings because the prescription sleep aid Ambien and other medications in Stewart's system put him in a zombie-like state of mind when he entered the nursing home.

The jury didn't buy that argument. It found Stewart guilty of eight counts of second-degree murder—a verdict that spared him the death penalty. Stewart was sentenced to 189–236 months on each murder count for a total of 126–157 years in prison, which was basically life in prison without the possibility of parole. He was sent to Marion Correctional Institution in North Carolina.

As for Garner, he finally reached his law enforcement goal. In 2011, he became a member of the North Carolina State Highway Patrol. Now the father of two, he and Stephanie still live in the town he loves—Carthage, North Carolina.

A HEART IN THE RIGHT PLACE

TROOPER FIRST CLASS NATHAN BRADLEY
Georgia State Patrol

One of the toughest duties of a law enforcement officer is informing the next of kin that a loved one was killed. Georgia State Trooper Nathan Bradley has delivered such heartbreaking notification to victims' relatives many times—and it never gets easier.

On October 31, 2015, when he drove up to a house to break the news to an unsuspecting family that two of its members had died in a car accident, he braced himself for the emotional toll it would inflict on the relatives—and on him.

Bradley had never met them before, and, in fact, had no idea who would answer the door. He was acutely mindful that what he would say, and how he would say it, would greatly affect the family's reaction in dealing with its grief. He reminded himself to express the right words, report the tragic facts, make eye contact, speak in a calm voice, and show his genuine compassion, which he had in abundance.

Everyone who knew the 24-year-old Georgia-born trooper was aware that he had a big, caring heart that matched his six-foot two-inch, 260-pound frame. After all, he grew up in a family that valued public service. His sister was a deputy and his brother was a firefighter.

Now, as Bradley walked up to the modest brick house, which was set in the woods off the very country road where the victims had been killed, he took a deep breath and knocked. He was about to change the lives of the people inside forever.

But what he discovered after the door opened sent him reeling . . . and changed his life, too.

Hours earlier, late in the afternoon on a foggy, rainy Halloween, Bradley was patrolling in his police cruiser about 50 miles east of Atlanta when he overheard dispatch talking to another trooper on the radio about a "single-vehicle wreck with possible fatalities." Bradley typed the location of the accident into his GPS—Broughton Road by the T intersection with Dykes Road near the Jasper-Morgan county line—and saw that he was only 20 minutes away. He let dispatch know that he was heading there to assist.

When Bradley arrived on scene, the first responders' vehicles were flashing blue, red, and amber lights, but he noticed emergency personnel weren't hustling around with their usual urgency—a telltale sign that the victims had been pronounced dead at the scene.

Off the shoulder, beyond a curve in the road, lay the battered and twisted wreckage of an SUV. The initial investigation revealed that the vehicle, a 2015 Dodge Journey, had been traveling westbound on Broughton Road when it skidded out of control at the curve, spun clockwise, and left the pavement. It careened into a ditch and then went airborne before the passenger side of the vehicle slammed into a tree. The SUV flipped over and came to rest on the driver's side. The crash was so violent that even though the two occupants were each wearing a seat belt, they were probably killed instantly.

When the bodies were removed, police found the victims' driver's licenses. The person behind the steering wheel was Donald Howard, 33; his passenger was Crystal Howard, 29. Both licenses had the same Newborn, Georgia, address, which was only a quarter mile away. Police assumed the victims were husband and wife.

After the field investigation was completed, Bradley arrived at the address to inform the next of kin, as was his official duty. The policy of the Georgia State Patrol (GSP) calls for a trooper in uniform to deliver a death notification in person, preferably with another trooper or official. In this case, Bradley was accompanied by a Morgan County sheriff's deputy and Deputy Coroner Rodney Little.

Bradley knocked and waited. Dogs barked. But no one answered for the longest time. Then a boy, dressed like horror movie character Freddy Krueger, cracked open the door.

Bradley flashed his badge, introduced himself, and asked, "Is there an adult I can speak to here?"

The boy, 13-year-old Justin Howard, shook his head and said, "My parents went to the store to buy candy and face paint. They should be back real soon."

"Is anybody else home?"

"Just my sister and brothers."

Bradley's heart began to break when he met Justin's giggling, happy siblings, who were all decked out in their Halloween costumes: ten-year-old Amiah as Dracula's daughter, eight-year-old Daimean as a wizard, and six-year-old Trayvion as a firefighting Ninja Turtle.

Justin explained that their parents had gone to the nearest Walmart, which was about 20 minutes away near Madison. "There's not enough red face paint to make Daimean into an angry wizard," Justin told Bradley. "The red was spread as far as it would go, but it looks mostly pink." He added that their parents planned to take them trick-or-treating in several of the nearby rural subdivisions.

Seeing how excited the children were about Halloween and knowing they were home alone, Bradley pulled his two comrades aside and said, "There's no way I'm telling the kids about their parents now. It's better for them if they hear the news from someone they know and love, who could be with them and help them through this. That would soften the blow and be more compassionate. Otherwise it might be too traumatic for the children if a stranger tells them their parents died."

Bradley asked Justin if there were any relatives, family friends, babysitters, or clergy members who lived nearby.

Justin shook his head. By now, the boy was becoming suspicious. "Trooper, will you be honest with me?" he asked Bradley. "Police don't come up and knock on doors unless something bad has happened. Why are you here?"

Bradley put his arm around Justin, looked him in the eye, and said, "I will be honest with you, Justin, but now is not the time for me to answer all your questions. I need to stay focused. Trust me, when the time is right, I will tell you everything. Can we shake on it?" The boy agreed, and the two shook hands.

While the coroner and deputy kept the kids company, Bradley went back to his cruiser, hunched over his police laptop, and scoured national databases, trying to find the closest relative. He discovered that Donald Howard had previous driver's licenses when he lived in other states, including Florida. Owners of licenses in that state can list a contact number in case of emergency. Fortunately, the state still kept a record of that information from Donald's old license. He had listed his mother, Stephanie Oliver, of Sarasota, Florida.

Only in extremely rare cases will troopers phone a victim's family member to report a loved one's death. Bradley knew this was one of those instances when he had to make that dreaded phone call. His anguish doubled when he gazed out the windshield and saw the three youngest children laughing and running around the yard in their costumes, totally oblivious that they were now orphans.

His heart ached for them. And his stomach churned for what he was about to do. He took a deep breath, picked up the phone, and called. "Hello, is this Stephanie Oliver?"

"Yes."

"I am Trooper Nathan Bradley of the Georgia State Patrol. Are Donald and Crystal Howard your son and daughter-in-law?"

"Yes," she replied, suspicion creeping into her voice. "What's this all about?"

"I regret to inform you that they were in a terrible wreck. Unfortunately, they did not survive the accident and were pronounced dead at the scene."

After a moment of silence, the 55-year-old woman verbally blasted Bradley because she didn't believe him and accused him of engaging in a sick joke. "I get that it's Halloween, but you need to get off my phone," she snapped. Then she cussed him out.

"Ma'am, I'm not pranking you," the trooper said. He told her the kids' names and ages and a few more basic facts about the accident. "The children are home alone other than me, a sheriff's deputy, and the deputy coroner."

He finally convinced her that he was telling the horrible truth and then waited patiently on the phone while Miss Oliver broke down in sobs of grief. When she regained her composure, she told him, "Oh, how I wish this had been just a cruel Halloween prank."

"Yes, I understand," Bradley said. "I wish there had been no reason for this call. Do you know of anyone here who can care for the children?"

"No, I'm the closest relative." She said she would drive from her home in Sarasota, which was nearly 500 miles away, to claim custody of the kids. For the eight-hour ride, she planned to bring a companion.

Knowing that Miss Oliver was emotionally devastated, Bradley told her to take some time to grieve first. "There's no urgency right this second," he said. "Don't drive until you can do so safely. I don't want you behind the wheel crying and end up crashing and putting yourself and others at risk. I'll make sure the state takes good care of the kids until you get here."

It was already dark outside, so he knew their grandmother wouldn't arrive until the wee hours of the morning at the earliest. Following police protocol, Bradley radioed dispatch to notify Family and Child Services. He was told that a social worker wouldn't be available for at least three hours and that he should take the children to the county jail, where they would stay until a state worker could care for them.

Bradley felt sick to his stomach. *These kids will soon learn they lost both parents and will spend their Halloween night in a county jail. That's just not right.* He wasn't the kind of trooper who could just drop them off, file his report, and call it a day.

Bradley conferred with Little, who was a former post commander with the GSP. "I'm torn," the trooper told him. "I know the protocol is to turn the kids over to child services, but I don't think that's in their best interests. They would want to know why, and I don't want to be the one to tell them. I can't drop a bomb on them and then bring them to the jail until child welfare comes and takes them away. That will only make things a lot worse for them. If I was a kid, I wouldn't want a cop to tell me. I would want a family member or someone I was close to. They have no one here. Besides, if they learn the truth tomorrow, on November 1 rather than today, I can salvage their Halloween and preserve all their Halloweens to come."

"So what are you saying?" Little asked.

"I want to care for them until their grandma shows up. Do you think I'll get in trouble with the department?"

"If the department tries to discipline you for taking responsibility for the children at a time like this, then it's not the Georgia State Patrol I know," Little replied. "You're doing a good thing, Nathan."

After telling dispatch that he would temporarily care for the children, Bradley experienced a brief bout of anxiety. *What am I going to do with them? I'm only 24 and never have been responsible for a child's life before. Now I'm suddenly in charge of four kids.* But that uneasiness quickly passed. *Just be yourself.*

The trooper went over to the children and asked, "Would you like to go out to eat with me?"

The younger ones shouted, "Yes!" But Justin said, "Our parents should be coming home any minute."

It's important to me not to lie to them. "I hear what you're saying, Justin. But I just learned that your grandmother will be meeting with us later tonight. She wants all of you to hang out with me until she gets here."

"It's so weird," Justin said in a tone indicating something wasn't right. "Why would Grandma be coming?"

"She wants to see y'all," Bradley replied.

The children piled into the cruiser and buckled up. To their delight and excitement, he turned on the siren and flashing lights, hoping that would distract Justin from any further questions. Justin complimented the trooper on his campaign cover (a wide-brim trooper's hat) and his two police ball caps. "Feel free to wear one of the caps," Bradley said. Justin donned the campaign cover.

"Okay, now, what would everyone like to eat?" Bradley asked the kids. They bombarded him with different suggestions. Bradley stopped at McDonald's in Covington and bought Amiah a large order of fries and Trayvion a Happy Meal at their request. Then he drove 10 miles to the nearest Burger King, which was in Conyers, because Daimean wanted a Whopper with onions. They all went inside, where Bradley ordered milkshakes for everyone, hoping to stall for time and salvage their Halloween. He paid for everything out of his own pocket.

"This is a real treat," Amiah told him. "We hardly ever go out to eat because our mom is such a great cook."

Bradley could feel his heart tear as he smiled and nodded. *I have the worst fake smile in the world. But I have to try to keep up a brave face.*

He was impressed with how well-behaved, engaging, and bright they were. They conversed on a variety of subjects— everything from the universe to the circus, their favorite foods to their favorite TV shows.

The trooper learned that Donald—better known as DJ— and Crystal had met in Germany when they were in the military. Donald had served in the United States Army for eight years, completing tours in Afghanistan and Iraq. He was honorably discharged after tearing his ACL, a severe injury to a major ligament of the knee. Donald was Justin's stepfather but the biological father to the other three children. Crystal was the biological mother to all the children.

Amazed at the maturity and intelligence of the kids, Bradley asked, "How did y'all get to be so smart?"

They explained they were homeschooled by their parents. Said Justin, "Our mother is the teacher, but our father is the principal." Everyone laughed.

Bradley noticed he was getting strange looks from other customers because he was a white cop eating with four mixed-race children in this predominantly black community. He talked to the Burger King store manager and brought her to tears when he explained there had been a tragedy in the kids' family, but they hadn't been told yet.

Because he was constantly on his cell phone, Bradley had to get up and leave the table several times, so the kindhearted manager kept the children company. Even though it was closing time, she told the trooper, "I'll keep it open as long as you want." She also insisted on giving the kids free ice cream.

While Bradley dealt with his chain of command on the phone, it was decided that he should bring the children to his barracks, GSP Post 46, south of Monroe. His supervisor, Corporal Richard Thacker, called to check up on Bradley. Touched by the heartrending situation, Thacker told him, "I'm bringing my wife and son to meet you and the children at the post."

Bradley returned to the table and said, "Hey, kids. After we're done eating ice cream, we're going to my post because there are a lot of people who want to meet you—and there'll be lots of candy." The kids cheered.

It had been an awful day for local law enforcement officers. In addition to the Howard fatalities, another couple had died in a car wreck caused by a drunk driver, and a motorcyclist was killed in an accident right in front of the state patrol post—all within a 20-mile radius. Bradley made sure the crash by the post had been cleared off before he would bring the children there.

When it was time to leave the restaurant, the kids, who were wearing paper Burger King crowns that the manager had given them, said good-bye to her. Justin hugged her in gratitude, explaining, "We give hugs in our family." One by one, the other children embraced her, too. Bradley told her, "You've been a great blessing to us all."

On their way to the post, Amiah blurted from the backseat, "You're the best cop ever!" Bradley struggled to accept the praise because of the terrible secret he was keeping from them—a secret that would soon turn their world upside down. "You turned an F-minus day into an A-plus night!"

He didn't quite understand her comment because she still didn't know the truth about her parents. *Maybe something else bad happened to her earlier*, he thought.

Amiah then asked the trooper, "Are you a fan of *Law & Order: SVU?*"

Bradley chuckled. "Aren't you a little young to be watching a show like that?"

"I like lots of police shows," she replied. "We record every episode, but our DVR ran out of space. Mom said she'll help me clear it of all the reruns."

After arriving at the post, Bradley gave them a tour of the place. He told them, "Everyone here accepts one another as family. The post is like a shared home, so don't be surprised if other people drop in to meet you."

At about 10:00 p.m., Thacker arrived with his family, bringing candy, popcorn, and several DVDs. Minutes later, as the children began watching *Monster House*, three area residents who had heard about the tragedy showed up at the post and handed the kids decorated goody bags filled with candy and small toys. The kids were elated. Soon Morgan County

Sheriff Robert Markley arrived with holiday buckets overflowing with candy. Amiah was awed because she had never met a real-life sheriff before. Markley talked to each child and then presented Justin with an honorary deputy's badge.

"Why do all these people want to meet us?" Justin asked.

"Oh, we're one big family," Bradley replied. "It's a holiday, and people are always coming by with treats, especially on Halloween."

Bradley called Miss Oliver on her cell phone to check on her. She told him that after his initial call, it took her two hours to recover from her immediate shock and sorrow. Because she was so late getting on the road, she and her companion weren't expected to arrive at the post until 6:00 or 7:00 a.m.

Bradley told the children that their grandmother wouldn't show up until morning, so the kids would spend the night at the post. It had several bedrooms, each with its own bathroom. The children took showers and were tucked into bed at about 2:00 a.m.

Staying up all night, Bradley called Miss Oliver every hour during her trip to make sure she was doing okay. She arrived early in the morning and then sat down with Bradley and wept as he answered her questions about the crash.

"What do I do now?" she asked him. "I've never experienced a loss like this."

"Neither have I," Bradley replied. He offered some basic guidance about consulting the coroner and making funeral arrangements.

She told him she wanted to wake the children up and immediately tell them about their parents' deaths.

"I strongly urge you to wait until you take them back to their house so you can enjoy their innocence one last time," the trooper suggested. "They'll be so happy to see you when they get up. But once you break the news, they'll look at you differently. Everything is going to change. It will never be the same again."

"You're right," she said with a sigh.

Miss Oliver then went over to each sleeping child and whispered a good morning. When the kids woke up, they jumped out of bed and hugged and kissed her. She broke down and cried. The children assumed her tears were from joy. But the tears were from knowing this happy moment would be the last bit of innocence the children would ever experience before she revealed the truth.

As Bradley escorted them to their grandmother's vehicle, Justin said, "Hopefully, Mom and Dad will be home by now."

Miss Oliver embraced Bradley and said, "I love you, I love you, I love you!" Then she whispered, "Thank you for preserving their innocence."

Wanting to remain in the kids' lives throughout the difficult days that awaited them, Bradley retrieved a trooper ball cap that he wore during his police academy training. On the underside of the bill, he penned a note, telling Justin, "You're a great person. Never change." Bradley also wrote down his cell phone number before handing him the cap. "This is for you to keep, Justin. Call me anytime."

Bradley then caught a few hours of sleep before starting his shift. Later that morning, after learning from Miss Oliver that she had told the children, Bradley drove over to their house. Justin answered the door, threw his arms around the trooper, and squeezed hard.

"Justin, I am so sorry for your loss," Bradley said.

"Yeah, it sucks. Why did both of them have to die?"

"That's a question that can't be answered. In my faith, I believe God has a purpose and that we shouldn't question God's actions."

Justin was quiet for a moment and then said, "Everything is going to be different from here on out."

"Yes, it is. You'll have to be the strong older brother. You'll have to be supportive of your younger siblings."

"I know," Justin said solemnly.

"I told you I would be honest with you when the time was right. Well, now is the time. It's important for me to be here because I have a lot of explaining to do, and I'll answer any questions you have."

Their conversation was interrupted when the other children came out and hugged the trooper. The younger kids were still having difficulty processing the tragic news.

After answering Justin's questions, Bradley learned that Miss Oliver was going to take the children back to her small home in Sarasota and put them in public school. The house would be incredibly cramped because her daughter and two other grandchildren were already living with her.

The move also meant that the kids would have to say good-bye to their six dogs, including two that were pregnant, because there was no room for pets at the Florida residence.

Two days later, Bradley received a call from Justin. "How are you holding up?" the trooper asked.

"I'm doing the best I can," the boy replied. "We went and saw the car, and then we went to the funeral home because Grandma wanted to see my parents' bodies. I didn't go inside."

"I'm proud of you for making that decision," the trooper said.

"The funeral home said it's going to cost $7,000 to get my parents from here to Florida. Grandma doesn't have any money, and we don't know anyone who does. I was hoping you could help us out."

"Justin, I wish I could. If I had the money, I would give it to you."

"The only other option is that they are buried here," said Justin. "The military will help pay for that but not for getting them to Florida."

It's not fair to have the kids living in Florida and their parents buried in Georgia. How often would they have a chance to visit the graves? "Let me see if I can raise you some money," Bradley told him. "I've never done anything like this before, but I know a lot of people. If we're lucky, I might collect a few hundred dollars. But we'll be thankful for whatever we can get."

That night, Bradley sat in front of his computer. The year before, after he had joined the GSP, he had deactivated his Facebook account, which had a sizeable number of friends. He activated the account and planned to ask for donations. But then he remembered there was a popular personal fund-raising website called GoFundMe.

Following the website's guidelines, he wrote a lengthy and heartfelt narrative about the crash that left four orphans. Below the title "Children Lost Both Parents in Wreck" was a photo of the kids during happier times. He asked for help in raising $7,000 for funeral expenses.

"The Georgia State Patrol has four core values: trust, fortitude, professionalism, and compassion," he wrote. "I'm hoping you can help me with the compassion part. All sums donated will be given directly to the family to be used for funeral costs. Any additional donations after our initial $7,000 goal is reached will be placed in a trust fund set up by the family and will be used to provide higher education to the four children."

He finished the write-up at 2:00 a.m., posted it on his Facebook page with a link to the crowd-sourcing site, and went to sleep with little expectation of raising the full amount. When he woke up and checked, he was surprised to see that people were already donating. Later that morning, more than $3,000 had been raised. *That's really impressive*, he thought.

People were sharing his write-up on social media and digging into their pockets to contribute. By the end of the day, he had raised far more than he ever dreamed possible—$37,000. And then, just like that, the heartbreaking tale of the Howard children went viral. Suddenly, Bradley's cell phone was blowing up with requests for interviews. Between arresting drunk drivers and writing speeding tickets, he was doing interviews for local, state, and national TV and radio shows, newspapers, and online magazines. He was receiving thousands of e-mails, many with offers to help. By the second day, donations had soared to nearly $150,000, then $300,000, and eventually skyrocketed over the next few days to almost a half million dollars. The Angel Foundation kicked in an additional $10,000.

Nearly 13,000 people donated on the GoFundMe site that Bradley set up, and 75,000 shared it on Facebook. The more money that was raised, the more pressure Bradley felt because he had never dealt with such a large sum. He spent his free time consulting with lawyers, financial planners, bankers, judges, and his supervisors. The money was soon put into special trust funds for the children's education and care, all under the management and supervision of a professional conservator.

Because of the money raised, the orphans were given an improved chance to succeed in life, all thanks to a trooper who did what he felt compelled to do, which was to follow his heart.

*   *   *

On November 14, 2015, the bodies of Donald and Crystal Howard were laid to rest at Sarasota National Cemetery in a funeral attended by their children, family, and friends.

The Howards' house in Newborn, Georgia, was rented out, and the children's dogs were given to adoptive families. The kids settled in to their new life in a small, cramped house in Sarasota with their grandmother, their aunt Sharlee Dismuke, and two cousins. Since their story went viral, they have felt the love and generosity of others from all walks of life. Strangers have sent them clothes, books, and toys.

Ivory Chevrolet, of Union City, Georgia, gave them a free 2014 Chrysler minivan worth $18,000. "Their story really touched us a lot," Joey Loesdale, who donated the vehicle and delivered it to them in Sarasota, told reporters. "I can't replace what the family has lost, but we can give them something today that makes them smile."

The Tampa Bay Buccaneers treated the four children and their relatives to VIP seats for a game against the Atlanta Falcons. Earlier, at a Bucs practice session, the kids met some of the football players and had their photos taken with them.

Busch Gardens in Tampa helped Daimean and Amiah celebrate their birthdays by giving all four kids, their friends, and relatives a free day at the theme park.

"This is like the whole nation has been so helpful, and we just don't know how to thank everybody," their aunt Sharlee said in 2016. "We just love everybody."

Asked how the kids have adjusted, she said, "They're doing okay. They have their moments when they talk about Mom and Dad, so I know they miss them."

The day after the Howards' funeral, Bradley married Stephanie Humphries in Auburn, Georgia. But that didn't mean he would ignore the children.

"I love them and will always be their friend," says the trooper, who keeps in touch regularly through phone calls and text messages. "I care a lot about them and want to watch them succeed. I don't want the tragedy to shadow them the rest of their lives."

He says that the whole experience with the Howard family has made him a better person. "I've become much more sensitive to what's going on in the lives of other people—including those I stop for traffic violations.

"Because of my job, I usually see people at their worst. But I've found through this tragedy that people in general are compassionate and caring and willing to help total strangers, orphans like Justin, Amiah, Daimean, and Trayvion. It opened my eyes to see just how good people can be."

ABOUT THE AUTHOR

Allan Zullo is the author of more than 100 nonfiction books on subjects ranging from sports and the supernatural to history and animals.

He has introduced Scholastic readers to the 10 True Tales series, gripping stories of extraordinary persons who have met the challenges of dangerous, sometimes life-threatening situations. Among the books in the series are *Heroes of Pearl Harbor*; *Vietnam War Heroes*; *World War I Heroes*; *World War II Heroes*; *War Heroes: Voices from Iraq*; *Battle Heroes: Voices from Afghanistan*; *Young Civil Rights Heroes*; *FBI Heroes*; and *Heroes of 9/11*. In addition, he has authored five books about the real-life experiences of young people during the Holocaust—*Survivors: True Stories of Children in the Holocaust*; *Heroes of the Holocaust: True Stories of Rescues by Teens*; *Escape: Children of the Holocaust*; *We Fought Back: Teen Resisters of the Holocaust*; and *Young Survivors of the Holocaust*.

Allan, the father of two grown daughters and the grandfather of five, lives with his wife, Kathryn, near Asheville, North Carolina. To learn more about the author, visit his website at www.allanzullo.com.